Becoming *a* Church *of* Lifelong Learners

THE GENERATIONS OF FAITH SOURCEBOOK

John Roberto

D0067364

TWENTY
THIRD 23rd
PUBLICATIONS

The research and development of the Generations of Faith Project and this book, *Becoming a Church of Lifelong Learners*, has been funded through a generous grant from the Lilly Endowment.

Cover art: "One Sacred Community" by Mary Southard, CSJ. Courtesy of www.ministryofthearts.org

Second printing 2006

Twenty-Third Publications, A Division of Bayard
One Montauk Avenue, Suite 200,
New London, CT 06320
(860) 437-3012 or (800) 321-0411
www.23rdpublications.com

ISBN-10: 1-58595-571-X
ISBN 978-1-58595-571-8

Library of Congress Catalog Card Number: 2005936951
Printed in the U.S.A.
The Scripture passages contained herein are from the *New Revised Standard Version of the Bible*, copyright ©1989, by the Division of Christian Education of the National Council of Churches in the U.S.A. All rights reserved.

Dedication

This book is dedicated to two groups of people who have been instrumental in my life. First, I dedicate this book to my own family of faith. To my mother, Anna, and to the memory of my father, John, who first formed me in the Catholic faith, and to my wife, Linda, and to Michael, Elizabeth, and Jessica who have journeyed with me in my ministry life over the past thirty years, thank you for your support and encouragement.

Second, I dedicate this book to all the pioneers of new approaches to faith formation. These are the people on whose shoulders we all stand. They are the people who inspired and mentored me through their vision of a better future for faith formation. A very special thanks to John Westerhoff, Kate Dooley, Charles Foster, and Maria Harris. This book and the Generations of Faith project seek to make their vision a reality today.

I also want to thank the staff of the Center for Ministry Development for their support and encouragement of my work. Thanks to Tom East, Joan Weber, Leif Kehrwald, Mariette Martineau, Cheryl Tholcke, Ann Marie Eckert, and Sean Lansing.

Contents

Introduction

The paradigm of faith formation in the Catholic Church in the United States is changing. The era in which parish faith formation was dominated by a classroom, schooling paradigm is ending. A new paradigm better suited to today's people and issues is emerging. It is an ancient-new paradigm with roots in the early Church. The new paradigm is lifelong, ecclesial faith formation, centered in the events of Church life, engaging people of all generations in parish intergenerational learning, and nurturing faith at home throughout the life cycle. It is a complete system of faith formation, not a new program. Only a comprehensive approach will be able to address the urgent needs of faith formation in the Catholic Church.

Becoming a Church of Lifelong Learners presents the research, vision, and practices that provide a foundation for lifelong faith formation. The first chapter analyzes the social-cultural context and identifies important trends having an impact on faith formation today. It explores current research on the religious beliefs and practices of American Catholics and the implications of this research on the future of faith formation. Chapter Two presents the vision of lifelong faith formation, grounded in the catechetical vision of the Catholic Church and the writings of leaders in religious education. Lifelong faith formation is proposed as a new paradigm for the Church. Chapters Three through Six present the four essential practices that make lifelong faith formation a reality in parish life:

1. events-centered systematic curriculum for the whole parish community,
2. events-centered intergenerational learning,
3. household faith formation, and
4. collaborative and empowering leadership.

While this book is written from a Roman Catholic perspective, I believe the vision and practices can be adapted for other Christian churches, especially the more liturgically-oriented mainline churches.

Becoming a Church of Lifelong Learners: The Generations of Faith Sourcebook has developed from ten years of research, development, and direct work with parishes across North America by the Center for Ministry Development. Generations of Faith is not a program. It is an approach to creating lifelong, intergenerational, events-centered faith formation. Parishes of all sizes and cultures—from small town parishes, to city parishes and large suburban parishes—have found the Generations approach works in their parish community.

The key to the Generations approach is that it builds on the strengths of a parish's current catechetical programming, while creating a lifelong faith formation plan and intergenerational learning programs that gather all the generations to learn together. Parishes customize the Generations approach to their parish community: to the mission of the parish, the needs of their people, the cultures in the parish, and the resources and facilities of the parish.

In 2001 the Center for Ministry Development received a multi-year grant from the Lilly Endowment to work with parishes across North America to implement a lifelong, intergenerational, events-centered approach to faith formation. Through the Generations of Faith project the Center has created workshops, online resources, and publications to support parishes in their work. The project's Web site, www.generationsoffaith.org, is a primary resource for helping parishes plan, implement, and conduct lifelong faith formation. As of January 2006, over 1200 parishes across the United States and Canada are working to incorporate lifelong, intergenerational, events-centered learning into their parish community.

Becoming a Church of Lifelong Learners is one of two publications from the Generations of Faith project. The second publication, *Generations of Faith Resource Manual: Lifelong Faith Formation for the Whole Parish Community*, is designed as a planning guide and workbook to help the parish community embrace the vision and practices of lifelong faith formation. *Generations of Faith Resource Manual* provides detailed processes and tools to move from vision to reality: fashioning a lifelong curriculum, implementing a lifelong curriculum plan, developing leaders for lifelong faith formation, and designing an events-centered learning plan (intergenerational learning and household faith formation).

Chapter One

Reading the Signs of the Times

Over the past forty years we have seen exciting developments in faith formation and learning in the Catholic Church. Parishes across the country have engaged in new ways to encourage Catholics of all ages to deepen their relationship with Jesus Christ and their understanding and practice of the Catholic faith. We have seen the re-introduction of the Rite of Christian Initiation of Adults; religious education programs for children and teens that are doctrinally sound and developmentally-appropriate; family-centered religious education programs, especially for sacramental preparation; youth ministry programs for teenagers; parish renewal programs such as RENEW and Disciples in Mission; adult education programs; small faith sharing groups, and Bible study groups, to name only a few.

But we also live in times that present tremendous new challenges for developing a Catholic way of life and sharing our Catholic faith with the next generation. Over the past forty years, American Catholics have experienced the gradual loss of a distinctive Catholic culture, held together by ethnicity, multi-generational families, national (ethnic) parishes, and Catholic schools, all set within a local neighborhood. Most Catholics born before 1960 grew up in this Catholic culture and can still vividly remember how they were literally immersed in the Catholic way of life 24/7, 365 days a year. This was a Catholicism grounded in community and tradition.

Today Catholics are not as immersed in Catholic culture and Catholic social networks as they once were. Sociologist Dean Hoge analyzes the situation in this way:

We believe that Catholicism's outsider status in nineteenth- and early twentieth-century America, the general compliance with hierarchical and institutional norms, and the formative power of Catholic culture in its religious and ethnic dimensions powerfully shaped Catholic identity....Today by contrast, personal choice and religious individualism are dominant. It is this situation—the transformation of Catholicism from a perceived church of obligation and obedience to a church of choice—that has accelerated dramatically in the wake of the 1960s....

This transformation continues today, driven in large part by an exaggerated individualism. Catholic identity construction in America's culture of choice is much less amenable to ecclesiastical control and institutional influence than in the past. (*Young Adult Catholics*, p. 225-226)

Faith formation today no longer exists in the interdependence of the ecology that nurtured people in the Catholic faith. All but gone are the overlapping support environments of Catholic, multi-generational families living together in the neighborhood where the parish was the center of Catholic and community life and the Catholic school provided an education for children. This was a world in which Catholics shared a common language of faith, sacramental symbols, parish experiences, and tradition.

We know that the context for faith formation is changing. How will the trends in society, culture, and Church affect faith formation today and in the future? How will these trends influence the development of a Catholic identity and Catholic way of life among all generations, but especially the new generations of Catholics? This chapter seeks to document several of the most important changes occurring in society and culture, in the Catholic Church, and in the religious profiles of American Catholic generations, and point to the implications of these changes for faith formation today and in the future.

Trends in Society and Culture

There is so much social and cultural change occurring within our country and world, it is hard to catch our breath, much less analyze the changes and their impact on faith formation. The following four themes describe changes that are having a profound impact on faith formation in local parishes. They are by no means the only forces affecting faith formation today, but they have a particular influence on the development of a Catholic identity and a Catholic way of life.

1. We live in a time of rapid social and cultural transformation, nationally and globally. We are living in a period of profound change characterized by increasing social, ethnic, cultural, and religious pluralism. Individuals and groups face unprecedented and overwhelming choices, strains in patterns of living, and unprecedented diversity in the people and factors shaping the context for choice. This great diversity makes the process of forming and sustaining a Catholic identity more difficult.

There is a lack of trust in authority generally and a particular disenchantment with groups formerly regarded as authoritative. These include government leaders, civic leaders, educational institutions, law enforcement, the justice system, and institutional religion. The authority of religious leaders has declined, as has people's loyalty to their faith communities and denominational identity.

There is a growing complexity and fragmentation in modern life. It seems that a growing number of organizations—economic, religious, educational, social, recreational—and their organized activities compete for the time and attention of people. Modern life is fragmented into ever smaller units which compete with one another for the participation and loyalty of people. It is very difficult today to develop a sense of coherence in one's life as people are engaged in such a wide diversity of activities.

The competing diversity of organizations and activities contribute to the growing separation of age groups and generations throughout society. More and more activities are targeted to a narrow range of ages or interest groups. As a society we have lost most of the settings in which all of the generations are engaged in meaningful activities together.

> ▶ How do we develop and sustain a Catholic identity and Catholic way of life in a world of increasing diversity, complexity, and age segregation, and with declining trust in authority and loyalty to communities?

2. We are a society of increasing secularization with a pluralism of value systems that especially affect the younger generations. Today's society has no dominant value system or model of social life. Instead, there are a variety of value systems that are often in conflict with one another.

There is no widely acknowledged authority positioned to influence or advocate today's values definitively. In this absence, the entertainment media has become the primary conveyor of our common culture, and with it, the main bearer of the values of a secular society. The values that today's media present, especially to the young, usually run counter to the Catholic faith and value system. These values are embedded in images that attract and seduce (think MTV and contemporary advertisements). Gone are the days when the Catholic worldview with its images, symbols, values, and traditions was the primary influence on Catholic children and teenagers. Instead, a Catholic identity and way of life is made difficult in a secular society that is so pervasive and hostile to Catholic values.

▶ How do we develop and sustain a Catholic identity and Catholic way of life in a secular, pluralistic society where the media is the primary conveyor of society's values?

3. *We live in an experienced-based, participative, interactive, image-driven, and connected culture.* Contemporary culture has shifted dramatically over the past several decades toward what many people call a "postmodern" culture. Everyone is immersed in the postmodern culture. While today's young adults, teenagers, and children have grown up in this culture and are "native" to it, the older generations have had to learn how to adjust and live in this "new" culture.

Take a moment to think about your everyday experience of today's culture. Have you ever frequented a Starbucks coffee shop, a Home Depot or Lowe's home improvement store, an REI (Recreational Equipment Inc.) store, or a Borders or Barnes and Noble bookstore? Each of these stores sell products, but the commodity is secondary to the experience they provide their customers. Starbucks creates an environment for coffee lovers complete with music, daily newspapers, tables, chairs, and sofas. They have even created their own language for ordering a cup of coffee, suited to the personal tastes of each individual. You are entering a community of coffee-lovers.

Borders and Barnes and Noble provide an experience for book-lovers, complete with a café, chairs and sofas, a children's section with regular programs, book club meetings, and book signings by authors. They have created a community of readers and a "neighborhood center" where it is not unusual for people to spend hours in the store. At each REI store people can experience the products in the store such as testing out climbing equipment on the multi-storied rock climbing wall or riding a bike on the track. REI has turned purchasing outdoor equipment into an experience. Even the aisles of the store resemble a hiking path. Home Depot and Lowe's stores have transformed home improvement into an experience. Each day these stores run numerous clinics to give people the experience (and confidence) to repair or improve their homes. Customers can try out products before they purchase them.

This cultural change is not limited to businesses. Children's museums, growing in popularity and number over the past twenty years, are experience centers. Any parent or grandparent who has taken children to a museum marvels at the way in which everything is participative and interactive, engaging all of the children's (and adults') senses. Learning about science is embedded in the experience.

Contemporary culture is experienced-based, participative, interactive, image-driven, and connected or relationship-centered. People of all ages, but especially the younger generations, bring these perspectives and expectations to their involvement and learning in the Church.

First, they want to experience life directly. They want to experience the story, the doctrine, the tradition, or the practice directly. It is a multi-sensory culture. People want to taste, touch, see, smell, and hear the story of Jesus and the tradition. It is through experience that they change. Leonard Sweet describes the connection to the Christian way of life this way:

> The Way is not a method or a map. The Way is an experience. Postmodern leaders are experience architects. Postmoderns come to church to explore: "Is it real?" "Give me an experience, and then I'll see whether or not I believe it." Try-before-you-buy postmoderns will not first find the meaning of faith in Christ and then participate in the life of the church. Rather, they will participate first and then discern the meaning of faith. In postmodern culture, the experience is the message. (*SoulTsunami*, p. 215)

Second, people want interactivity and participation. They perceive, comprehend, and interact with the world as much as participants as observers. In fact, people do not give their undivided attention to much of anything without it being interactive.

> It is no longer enough to possess things or to enjoy positive events. One now has to be involved in bringing those events to pass or brokering those things into the home. People want to participate in the production of content, whatever it is....
>
> Postmoderns are not simply going to transmit the tradition or culture they've been taught. They won't take it unless they can transform it and customize it. Making a culture their own doesn't mean passing on a treasure that they've inherited, but inventing and engineering their own heirloom out of the treasures of the past. (*Post-Modern Pilgrims*, p. 58-59, 62)

Third, contemporary culture is image-driven. We used to live in a word-based, print culture. We now live in a world where story and metaphor are at the heart of spirituality. "Propositions are lost on postmodern ears, but metaphor they will hear; images they will see and understand." Leonard Sweet describes one of the implications of the image-driven culture in this way:

> Cultures are symbol systems, intricate, interwoven webs of metaphors, symbols, and stories. What holds the culture of the church together—the metaphors it offers, the symbols it displays, the stories it tells? The church seems to have lost the plot to the "stories of Jesus." Could it be because the redemption story was told in the modern era more by "creeds" and "laws" than by "parables"—narrative-wrapped images? (*Post-Modern Pilgrims*, p. 88-89)

Fourth, people hunger for connection and community. Relationship issues stand at the heart of postmodern culture. As John Naisbitt noted in *Megatrends*, the more high tech the society becomes, the more people will seek high touch (relationships). The more impersonal the society becomes, the deeper the hunger for relationships and community. Once again Leonard Sweet notes,

> In the midst of a culture of communal anorexia, there is a deepening desire for a life filled with friends, community, service, and creative and spiritual growth. The Church must provide its people with a moral code, a vision of what gives life value, and an experience of embeddedness in a community to which one makes valuable contributions. Personal relationships are key in postmodern ministry....The church must help people build a communal life of deep and rich personal relationships. (*SoulTsunami*, p. 221)

The implications for faith formation are many. Robert Webber, quoting Parker Palmer, suggests that the most appropriate approach to education and nurture in a postmodern world is "a slow, subtle, nearly unconscious process of formation, something like the way a moving stream shapes the rocks over the long passage of time." Webber summarizes the postmodern shift in education when he writes,

> In the postmodern world education will shift from the passing down of information to the passing down of wisdom through experience. Christian truth, which was regarded as propositional, intellectual, and rational will be experienced as an embodied reality. Faith will be communicated through immersion into a community of people who truly live the Christian faith. The corporate commu-

nity will communicate through its depth of commitment, through hospitality, and through images such as baptism, the importance of Scripture, the significance of eucharistic celebration, and the feasts and fasts of the Christian year. These events will shape the imagination of the believer and provide transcendent points of reference that bring meaning to the cycle of life. The meaning of the stories, symbols, cycles of time, and audiovisual experiences of faith may become the center for thoughtful discussion and application in the small group and stimulate both an intellectual and emotional knowing. (*Ancient-Future Faith*, p. 155)

▶ How can faith formation become more experiential, participative, interactive, and image-driven? How can faith formation build community and connection among all parishioners?

▶ How can we help people touch, taste, see, smell, and hear the story of Jesus and the Catholic tradition?

4. *We live in a detraditionalized society where received traditions no longer provide meaning and authority in everyday life.* Diana Butler Bass in her book, *The Practicing Congregation*, describes detraditionalization as "a set of processes...whereby received traditions no longer provide meaning and authority in everyday life" (p. 28). We live in a society where the force of tradition no longer offers personal or spiritual security. People have lost faith in what the tradition has to offer. They do not value tradition and its wisdom. This is true not only for the traditions of family and society, but also of the Catholic faith. Bass, quoting Paul Heelas, a British sociologist, continues,

> "Detraditionalization entails," Heelas explains, "that people have acquired the opportunity to stand back from, critically reflect upon, and lose their faith in what the tradition has to offer. They have to arrive at a position where they can have their own say. Theorists of detraditionalization argue that organized culture—sustained voices of moral and aesthetic authority serving to differentiate values, to distinguish between what is important and what is not, to facilitate coherent, purposeful, identities, life plans or habits of the heart—has disintegrated." Thus detraditionalization is not only a real word: it is the lived reality of millions of people in today's world. (*The Practicing Congregation*, p. 30)

We see the processes of detraditionalization directly influencing the Church's efforts to nurture a Catholic identity, pass on the tradition, and develop a Catholic way of life in each new generation. Today, anyone involved in teaching the Catholic tradition does so in the face of the forces of detraditionalization.

Despite the power of detraditionalizing forces, "individuals—and congregations—are responding to the larger cultural results of modern fragmentation by creating communities that provide sacred space for the formation of identity and meaning, the construction of 'pockets' of connectedness to the long history of Christian witness and practice in a disconnected world" (*The Practicing Congregation*, p. 50). This is the process of *re*traditioning.

Diana Butler Bass notes that "retraditioning implies reaching back to the past, identifying practices that were an important part of that past, and bringing them to the present where they can reshape contemporary life." We can no longer assume that parishioners know the Catholic story and tradition. It must be imaginatively told, retold, and enacted, so that tradition becomes a living thing. "Retraditioning challenges churches to model a particular way of life; communities of practice that forge, express, and bear certain traditions. Thus, these congregations both carry and craft tradition in intentional ways" (*The Practicing Congregation*, p. 53).

▶ How do we provide sacred space for the formation of identity and meaning, connected to the long history of Christian witness and practice?

▶ How do we re-claim the Catholic tradition so that it can reshape the lives of communities and individuals?

Trends in Church Life

There are a number of trends in Church life that are having a direct impact on developing a Catholic identity and Catholic way of life today. Among the trends that need to be of special concern to Catholic leaders are:

- the steady erosion in Mass attendance over the past fifty years;
- the decline in the number of marriages in the Church and the increase in interfaith marriages;
- the diminishing involvement of families and the younger generations with the Catholic community and the Catholic way of life;
- the decline in religious traditions and practices at home;
- the inability of parishes to keep people engaged in Church life and catechesis after the celebration of first Eucharist, first reconciliation, and confirmation, and/or the completion of children's catechesis in eighth grade.

Mass Attendance

Mass attendance has declined steadily from the 1950s, when seventy-five percent of Catholics went to Mass every week, to now, when only one-third attend weekly. A Center for Applied Research in the Apostolate (CARA) poll conducted in September 2004, estimates that thirty-two percent of Catholics attend Mass every week. This reflects a drop from 1987 when forty-four percent attended weekly and from 1999 when thirty-seven percent attended weekly. This decline has been steeper among the younger generations (only twenty-six percent of young adults age 27-44 attend Mass weekly; only fifteen percent of 18-26 year olds) than oldest generations (about sixty percent of whom still attend weekly). As the size of the oldest generation decreases in the coming decade, they will be replaced by post-Vatican II Catholics who are attending Mass with much less frequency (see Table 1 for more information).

Declining Mass attendance is the tip of the iceberg. Under the water are ominous trends. Declining Mass attendance means that baptized Catholics are having less contact and involvement with the Catholic community and the Catholic way of life. This does not bode well for the future. Baptized Catholics are drifting away from core Catholic practice and one wonders how long you can maintain a Catholic imagination without regular contact with the sacramental life of the Church.

▶ What will inspire Catholics in a positive way to re-embrace the Mass, this core practice of the Catholic tradition?

Marriage

First, we know that young Catholics are marrying later and beginning families later than their parents or grandparents did. For many, this may mean that there are ten or more years after finishing high school before they marry and then several more years before they have their first child.

Second, although a majority of marriages still take place in the Church, the percentage of marriages taking place outside the Church is increasing (from no more than ten percent among pre-Vatican II Catholics to as many as one-third of post-Vatican II Catholics). Even those who marry other Catholics are increasingly not marrying in the Church.

Third, interfaith marriages continue to increase, from twenty-four percent among pre-Vatican II Catholics to forty percent among post-Vatican II Catholics. Fifty percent of all non-Latino Catholic marriages are now to non-Catholics. Increasing numbers of Catholics marrying non-Catholics are doing so outside the Church.

If the above trends continue, they will have serious ramifications for the future.

- If the length between high school and marriage continues to be a decade or more and if only fifteen percent of today's young adults (18-26) attend Mass weekly, can we assume that they are going to return to the Church to be married and begin active participation in Church life?

- If the length of time between marriage and the birth of the first child continues to widen, can we assume that young couples are going to bring their first child for baptism in the Church and become active in Church life?

- If the trend of marrying outside of the Church continues, can we assume that these couples will "come back" to the Church to have their children baptized?

- If couples do not marry in the Church and/or do not bring their children to be baptized, can we assume they are going to bring their children to religious education classes and preparation for first Eucharist and first reconciliation?

▶ How can we engage single young adults, married couples in the first years of marriage, and new parents with young children in the life of the faith community and in continuing faith formation?

▶ How can we provide faith formation that addresses the needs of families, especially interfaith families, and helps them build family faith sharing traditions and practices at home?

Participation and Practice

Research findings and pastoral experience point to the fact that the Church is experiencing a decline in the involvement of families and the younger generations with the Catholic community and the Catholic way of life. Sunday Mass attendance is only one indicator, but if people are not coming to Mass, what is the likelihood they are participating in the programs, community life, and ministries of the parish? James Davidson and his colleagues have analyzed participation rates and they conclude that using religious practice as a criterion, one could say with fairness that participation in Catholic community life is off about thirty-five to forty-five percent since the 1950s. All other things being equal, it is reasonable to predict that Catholics will be less attached to and involved in the Church twenty years from now as the pre-Vatican II generation dies and the post-Vatican II generation increases.

Complicating this picture is the inability of parishes to keep people engaged in parish life and continuing faith formation after the celebration of first Eucharist, first reconciliation, confirmation, and/or the completion of children's catechesis in eighth grade. Even while children and teens are participating in catechetical programs, the majority do not attend Mass weekly. And these are the people who are participating in the parish's catechetical program. There seems to be little or no connection between participation in a catechetical program and participation in parish life, especially Sunday Mass.

We also see a decline in religious traditions and practices at home. There are a variety of reasons for this, such as the complexity and busyness of everyday life, but one of the major reasons is the religious literacy and religious experience of today's parents. Many parents did not grow up in families where they experienced religious traditions and practices. Many were away from the Church for ten or more years before returning with their children for first Eucharist or the start of catechetical programming in first grade. They simply do not have the fluency with the Catholic tradition or the confidence to share it with their children.

If these three trends continue, we will see less and less contact and involvement with the Catholic community and Catholic way of life, and the continuing decline of Catholic traditions and practices at home. This is hardly a hope-filled future.

▶ How can faith formation re-engage people in the life of the faith community and provide continuous faith formation throughout life?

▶ How can faith formation empower and equip families to develop a community of faith and practice at home?

Trends in the Faith Life of Catholic Generations

Every six years since 1987, James Davidson, Dean Hoge, William D'Antonio, and their colleagues have studied American Catholic generations. Their one-of-a-kind research has provided invaluable insights into the faith and practice of American Catholics. They are documenting the changing face of the four generations of American Catholics.

Demographically, Catholics are divided into three broad groups:

17%   Pre-Vatican II generation (born in or before 1940)

33%   Vatican II generation (born between 1941-1960)

49%   Post-Vatican II generation (born since 1961, including Generation X and millennials)

Overall, they report that U.S. Catholics, who exhibited extraordinarily high levels of commitment to the Church and compliance with Church teachings in the 1950s, continue to experience God's presence in their lives. At the same time, they are less attached to the Church, less likely to participate in the sacraments and traditional practices, more likely to distinguish between teachings they consider core (and tend to accept), such as the Real Presence and Mary as the Mother of God, and the ones they consider peripheral (and tend to disagree with), such as birth control. And they show no signs of returning to earlier levels of religious orthodoxy.

The research team identified a number of important trends. They found that among American Catholics, there is

- a persistent sense of being Catholic;
- a continuing belief in core teachings such as the Trinity, incarnation, resurrection, and Real Presence of Christ in the Eucharist;
- less religious practice, from higher levels among pre-Vatican II Catholics to lower levels of behavioral involvement among young Catholics;
- less attachment to the Church as institution;
- a movement from obedience to personal autonomy;
- increasing emphasis on conscience as the locus of authority regarding sexuality and reproductive issues.

The research team organized their 2005 findings into several categories. We will briefly examine four areas of the research findings and their implications for faith formation:

1. center of Catholic identity,
2. boundaries of Catholic identity,
3. generational differences, and
4. religious literacy.

1. Center of Catholic Identity

When asked what they consider most central, authentic, and important in being Catholic, eighty-four percent of Catholics ages eighteen and older identified helping the poor and belief in Jesus' resurrection from the dead;

seventy-six percent noted sacraments, such as Eucharist; and seventy-four percent said the Catholic Church's teaching about Mary as the Mother of God. These are clearly at the center of Catholic identity for all generations of Catholics (see Table 2 for more information).

In a 1997 study of Catholic young adults (ages 20-39) who had been confirmed as teenagers, Dean Hoge and his colleagues found very similar findings. When asked, "How essential is each of these elements to your vision of what the Catholic faith is?" young adults identified very similar elements as the 2005 study. The most important beliefs included the belief that God is present in the sacraments (65%), the belief that Christ is really present in the Eucharist (58%), charitable efforts toward helping the poor (58%), devotion to Mary (53%), and belief that God is present in a special way in the poor (52%).

How do these two surveys help us understand Catholic identity today? First, the researchers conclude that creedal beliefs are the main boundary markers of the faith: belief in Jesus' resurrection and belief in the presence of God in the sacraments, especially the Real Presence of Christ in the Eucharist. In addition, Catholics identify helping the poor and concern for social justice as essential to their Catholic identity.

Second, whatever the alienation of Catholics may be on some items of Catholic teaching, such as moral teachings, their imagination is still Catholic. In his book, *The Catholic Imagination*, Andrew Greeley identifies the three main areas of Catholic imagination: sacramentality, community, and hierarchy. It is clear that the strongest components of Catholic identity for American Catholics, and young adults in particular, are sacramental, community, and Marian. In the young adult survey, hierarchy is also present, since almost half of the respondents think that having a pope is essential.

In their summary of the research in *Young Adult Catholics*, Hoge and his colleagues offer this assessment:

> There are positive signs of young adult Catholic vitality today. Most young adults like being Catholic and cannot imagine themselves being anything other than Catholic. The overwhelming majority see the sacraments and devotion to Mary as essential to the Catholic faith. Some want to play a more active role in the Church. Most consider themselves spiritual, pray regularly, and support the Church's social mission.
>
> Young adult Catholics differ from mainline Protestants in that they (especially Latinos) have a stronger ethnic identity, a stronger identification with their church, and a more basic feeling that

Catholicism is the "real thing." They see Catholicism as the oldest and most central expression of Christianity, in continuity with the apostolic tradition and hallowed by the ages. Catholics seem to have a "glue" that Protestants do not have. They see Catholicism as a basic part of their being. In spite of beliefs and practices that are sometimes divergent, they remain "Catholic." Many young adult Catholics also take pride in the global dimensions of Catholicism and in the media visibility of a pope (John Paul II) whose personal integrity and firmness on moral and ethical questions are admired and respected even when not always followed personally. (p. 218-219)

2. Boundaries of Catholic Identity

A second question that researchers have asked American Catholics since 1987 concerns what is necessary to be a good Catholic. The findings are remarkably consistent since the first survey in 1987. The most essential requirements for being a good Catholic include believing that Jesus physically rose from the dead, believing that in the Mass the bread and wine become the body and blood of Jesus, and donating time or money to help the poor. Obeying the Church's teachings on abortion, birth control, and divorce and remarriage are among the least imperative requirements for being a good Catholic. Seventy-six percent of American Catholics agree that you can be a good Catholic without going to church every Sunday (see Table 4 for more information).

Two other questions in the 2005 survey reveal how Catholics perceive boundaries. The first question concerns the truth of Catholicism: fifty-six percent agreed with the statement that "Catholicism contains a greater share of truth than other religions do." This tells us that about one-half of American Catholics are uncertain about the greater truth of Catholicism as a defining boundary. Older persons tended to agree more—sixty-one percent of Catholics sixty-five or over did so, compared to forty-three percent of those twenty-six or younger.

The second question explores the belief-practice issue: eighty-eight percent agree that "How a person lives is more important than whether he or she is a Catholic." This tells us that the vast majority of Catholics take more seriously a person's behavior than his or her professed creed or church membership. In effect, a Catholic's behavior is actually a more consequential boundary. On this statement, both young and old agreed, according to Dean Hoge, in "Center of Catholic Identity" (*National Catholic Reporter*, September 30, 2005).

These survey findings contribute to an understanding of how American Catholics view Catholic identity today. They are not statements of theology, only of respondents' view of Catholic identity. In the words of Dean Hoge, "All we can say is that we have tried to measure the current reality. Knowing the actual situation on the ground is useful, since it tells us what is empowering and nourishing about the lived faith."

He continues, "This research also gives a hint about change. From the research we have seen, the center is not shifting. The main change is in the boundaries—they are now fairly vague and porous, and they are slowly becoming more so over time. Boundaries that make no sense to young adults cannot be maintained over the long haul. More meaningful boundaries need to be defined and explained."

3. Generational Differences

There is broad agreement across the generations on the core elements of the creed and Catholic beliefs that have been part of the Catholic tradition for centuries. These core elements are the single most important basis of Catholic unity. They are the glue that holds Catholics together. They are the reasons why Catholics remain loyal to the Church, even when they disagree with it on other matters.

Social teachings represent another area of common ground. Most Catholics embrace the principle of concern for the poor and helping the needy. Parishioners may disagree on specific social policies, but very few reject the Church's emphasis on a "preferential option for the poor" and Church involvement in social justice issues. The differences across generations occur over the level of commitment to the Church and on moral teachings, especially in the areas of sexuality and gender. Overall, we can say that parishioners' views of faith and morals form a rather loosely integrated Catholic worldview. William D'Antonio analyzes the generational differences in this way,

> Our surveys suggest that people are adrift in different degrees across the generations. The young and middle-aged are different from the older pre-Vatican II generation in being less committed to parish life and Church involvement, and in emphasizing much more the role of individual conscience in the face of moral issues. In addition, the 2005 survey found a split in the youngest generation in that the very youngest (ages 18-26) were even less Church-involved and more oriented to conscience than older young adults.
>
> These generational differences occur not because people change as

they age but because young adults enter the adult population at a different place. They are already different when pollsters first encounter them at age 18, 20, or 22. Sociologists call this pattern "cohort replacement," which means that older people are replaced in the total population by young cohorts whose life history is necessarily different from the outgoing cohort or generation. This produces change overall even though the great majority of individuals within the cohort don't change much during their adult lives. Each generation is relatively constant, yet each is distinctive. ("Generational Differences," *National Catholic Reporter*, September 30, 2005)

In short, any hope for a natural "rebound" or "U-shape effect," with younger Catholics embracing views and practices similar to their grandparents' generation (pre-Vatican II), is not justified by the research. Rather, it appears that there is a linear trend away from conventional religious sensibilities, with the youngest Catholics being the least inclined to maintain traditional faith practices and morals.

In their 1997 book, *The Search for Common Ground*, James Davidson and his colleagues underscored these generational differences and the clear trend that the post-Vatican II Catholics will not return to traditional levels of religious belief and practice on their own.

While some of the differences are due to age, to an even greater extent, these differences reflect the different experiences that age groups have during their formative years. Catholics raised in the 1930s and '40s, 1950s and '60s, and 1970s and '80s were raised in very different societal conditions. While the oldest cohort experienced economic depression and World War II during its formative years, the middle cohort experienced the prosperity of the post-war years and the social movements of the 1960s; the youngest cohort experienced the economic polarization and social dilemmas of the last 20 years. The cohorts also experienced three very different types of Catholicism: the pre-Vatican II Church, the Vatican II Church, and the post-Vatican II Church. As a result, they learned very different approaches to religion in their lives. Other research on cohort effects also suggests that learning experiences during people's formative years affect their religious outlooks through their lives. When and if today's young Catholics become more involved in the Church, they will bring with them the social and religious outlooks they learned during their formative years. Their approaches to faith and morals will never be the same as those currently held by their parents and grandparents.

These cohort differences point to declining levels of childhood religiosity, closeness to God, and commitment to the Church. Young Catholics are less religious in childhood than their parents and grandparents; they report few experiences of God's presence in their lives; and they are less committed to the Church. Unless steps are taken, these trends portend a future of dwindling faithfulness among young Catholics, diminishing awareness of God's presence in the lives of Catholic adults, further erosion of Catholic identity, and a declining sense that the Church is worth supporting. These trends, in turn, signal a continuation of recent tendencies to disagree with traditional faith and morals and to embrace religious ideas that are incompatible with Church teachings. (p. 203-204)

4. Religious Literacy

To see how widespread religious illiteracy is in today's Church, the research team asked American Catholics to agree or disagree with the following statement: "You often feel that you cannot explain your faith to others." James Davidson reports that while this item is only one of many possible indicators of illiteracy, the responses are instructive. Forty-nine percent of American Catholics said that they cannot explain their faith to other people, while fifty-one percent disagreed and said they could explain their faith to others. Those who are better educated, such as college graduates, and more involved in the Church, such as those who attend Mass two to three times a month, are least likely to say they cannot explain their faith to others.

Are there generational differences among those who cannot explain their faith to others? The percent who cannot explain their faith to others actually decreases as you move from the pre-Vatican II generation to the post-Vatican II generation: pre-Vatican II—fifty-nine percent, Vatican II—forty-nine percent, post-Vatican II (Gen X)—forty-four percent, and post-Vatican II (millennials)—forty-seven percent. "Religious illiteracy is highest among pre-Vatican II Catholics. It is the older, not the younger, Catholics who have the hardest time explaining their faith to others" ("Challenging Assumptions about Young Catholics," American Catholics Survey, *National Catholic Reporter*, September 30, 2005).

What are we to make of these findings? Religious illiteracy appears to be rather widespread and affects all four generations. It is not a youth or young adult problem. Religious literacy is an ongoing concern, and efforts to increase religious literacy should be oriented to Catholics of all ages, not just young adults.

Conclusions

What can we conclude from these research findings? The 2005 research, supported by the prior three studies (1987, 1993, and 1999), raise critical issues of Catholic identity and Catholic practice that the Church and faith formation need to address. These conclusions form an agenda for faith formation today and in the future.

1. The center of Catholic identity is creedal beliefs and helping the poor/concern for social justice. Catholics are more likely to distinguish between teachings they consider core (and tend to accept) and ones they view as peripheral (and tend to disagree with).

2. The boundaries of Catholic identity are now fairly vague and porous, and they are slowly becoming more so over time. Boundaries that make no sense to the post-Vatican II generations cannot be maintained over the long haul.

3. There has been an uncoupling of faith and Church life, also Catholic identity and attachment to the Church. Catholics are more likely to identify with the Catholic faith than the institutional Church. For many, Catholicism is less a matter of core identity and more a matter of personal option; it is more individualistic. We see this especially within the post-Vatican II generations.

4. Catholics, especially young adults, are less attached to the Church and less likely to participate in sacraments and traditional devotional practices.

5. The Vatican II and post-Vatican II generations of Catholics show no signs of returning to the early levels of religious orthodoxy and practice demonstrated by the pre-Vatican II generation.

6. Religious literacy is a problem across all generations. Across generations, but especially among post-Vatican II generations, people have a difficult time articulating a coherent sense of Catholic identity. While young adults like being Catholic, they are not sure what is distinctive about Catholicism, what Catholic heritage actually means, and what are Catholicism's core narratives.

The summary by Dean Hoge and his colleagues in *Young Adult Catholics* captures the urgency of our present situation. The trends within the post-Vatican II generations of Catholics are clear and urgent.

> For many young adults, Catholic identity is weak, focused outside the institutional Church, and only moderately central to their lives. The implications are portentous. If many young adults now believe

that Catholicism is simply another denomination, that it "doesn't really matter that much whether you're Catholic or not," that there is nothing unique or distinctive about Catholicism, or that all that really counts is a generic Christian lifestyle, Catholicism's institutional vitality, public witness, and capacity to retain its young are in jeopardy. Weak centrality of Catholic identity will have a snowballing effect on a variety of behaviors adversely impacting the Church, including moral choices, choices about marriage partners, child rearing practices, Catholic schooling, church attendance, and others. Nor can one assume that marriage will continue to serve as a port of entry (or reentry) into the Church. Young adult Catholics are waiting later to marry and therefore experiencing longer periods of disconnectedness from the Church. Fifty percent of all non-Latino Catholic marriages are now to non-Catholics. Increasing numbers of Catholics marrying non-Catholics are doing so outside the Church. These trends will have serious ramifications for the future. (*Young Adult Catholics*, p. 228-229)

The Impact of the Trends

It is hard not to be overwhelmed by the trends affecting faith formation in the Catholic Church. These trends create a sense of urgency to which we need to respond to now. There is much at stake. Dean Hoge says it very well when he writes, "Without a distinct sense of identity, a shared faith and some common elements of religious life relating to sacraments, discipleship, community, tradition, and hierarchy, there is no Catholicism" (*Young Adult Catholics*, p. 229).

The analysis of these trends makes it clear that our faith formation efforts need to respond to the reality of the current situation in the American Catholic Church. It is painful to face these trends. It is difficult to change our current ways of doing things, but that is what we are being called to do. How can parish faith formation in the Catholic Church respond to the urgency of our present and future situation? We now turn our attention to this question.

Works Cited

Bass, Diana Butler. **The Practicing Congregation**. Herndon, VA: Alban Institute, 2004.

D'Antonio, William, James Davidson, Dean Hoge, and Mary Gautier. "Survey of U.S. Catholics." **National Catholic Reporter**, September 30, 2005.

D'Antonio, William, James Davidson, Dean Hoge, and Katherine Meyer. **American Catholics**. Walnut Creek, CA: Rowman and Littlefield, 2001.

Davidson, James, Andrea Williams, Richard Lamanna, Jan Stenftenagel, Kathleen Mass Weigert, William Whalen, and Patricia Wittberg. **The Search for Common Ground**. Huntington, IN: Our Sunday Visitor, 1997.

Hoge, Dean, William Dinges, Mary Johnson, and Juan Gonzales. **Young Adult Catholics**. Notre Dame, IN: University of Notre Dame Press, 2001.

Sweet, Leonard. **SoulTsunami: Sink or Swim in the New Millennium Culture**. Grand Rapids, MI: Zondervan, 1999.

———. **Post-Modern Pilgrims: First Century Passion for the 21st Century World**. Nashville: Broadman and Holman Publishers, 2000.

Webber, Robert. **Ancient-Future Faith**. Grand Rapids, MI: Baker Books, 1999.

For Further Reading

Bass, Diana Butler. **The Practicing Congregation**. Herndon, VA: Alban Institute, 2004.

Cimino, Richard and Don Lattin. **Shopping for Faith: American Religion in the New Millennium**. San Francisco: Jossey-Bass, 1998.

D'Antonio, William, James Davidson, Dean Hoge, and Mary Gautier. "Survey of U.S. Catholics." **National Catholic Reporter**, September 30, 2005.

D'Antonio, William, James Davidson, Dean Hoge, and Katherine Meyer. **American Catholics**. Walnut Creek, CA: Rowman and Littlefield, 2001.

Davidson, James, Andrea Williams, Richard Lamanna, Jan Stenftenagel, Kathleen Mass Weigert, William Whalen, and Patricia Wittberg. **The Search for Common Ground**. Huntington, IN: Our Sunday Visitor, 1997.

Greeley, Andrew. T**he Catholic Revolution: New Wine, Old Wineskins, and the Second Vatican Council**. Berkeley, CA: University of California Press, 2004.

———. **The Catholic Imagination**. Berkeley, CA: University of California Press, 2000.

Hoge, Dean, William Dinges, Mary Johnson, and Juan Gonzales. **Young Adult Catholics**. Notre Dame, IN: University of Notre Dame Press, 2001.

Kitchens, Jim. **The Postmodern Parish**. Herndon, VA: Alban Institute, 2003.

Miller, Rex. **The Millennium Matrix: Reclaiming the Past, Reframing the Future of the Church**. San Francisco: Jossey-Bass, 2004.

Pine, Joseph B. and James H. Gilmore. **The Experience Economy**. Boston: Harvard Business School Press, 1999.

Steinfels, Peter. **A People Adrift: The Crisis of the Roman Catholic Church in America**. New York: Simon and Schuster, 2003.

Sweet, Leonard. **SoulTsunami: Sink or Swim in the New Millennium Culture**. Grand Rapids, MI: Zondervan, 1999.

— — —. **Post-Modern Pilgrims: First Century Passion for the 21st Century World**. Nashville: Broadman and Holman Publishers, 2000.

Webber, Robert. **Ancient-Future Faith**. Grand Rapids, MI: Baker Books, 1999.

Table 1. Attend Mass Weekly or More				
	Pre-Vatican II Generation (born in or before 1940)	Vatican II Generation (born 1941-1960)	Post-Vatican II Generation (born 1961-1979)	Millennial Generation (18-26 year olds only)
1987	58%	40%	30%	
1993	63%	42%	27%	
1999	64%	42%	27%	
2005	60%	35%	26%	15%

"AMERICAN CATHOLICS SURVEY," NATIONAL CATHOLIC REPORTER, SEPTEMBER 30, 2005

Table 2. Center of Catholic Identity

What is most central, authentic, and important in being Catholic?

MOST IMPORTANT

84%	Helping the poor
84%	Belief in Jesus' resurrection from the dead
76%	Sacraments, such as Eucharist
74%	The Catholic Church's teaching about Mary as the Mother of God
54%	Having a regular daily prayer life
50%	Participation in devotions, such as Eucharistic adoration or praying the Rosary
47%	The Catholic Church's teachings that oppose same-sex marriage
47%	Church involvement in activities directed toward social justice
44%	The Catholic Church's teachings that oppose abortion
42%	The teaching authority claimed by the Vatican
35%	The Catholic Church's teachings that oppose the death penalty
29%	A celibate male clergy

"AMERICAN CATHOLICS SURVEY," NATIONAL CATHOLIC REPORTER, SEPTEMBER 30, 2005

Table 3. Catholic Young Adults

How essential is each of these elements to your vision of what the Catholic faith is?

VERY IMPORTANT

65%	Belief that God is present in the sacraments
58%	Belief that Christ is really present in the Eucharist
58%	Charitable efforts toward helping the poor
53%	Devotion to Mary

52%	Belief that God is present in a special way in the poor
48%	Having religious orders of priests, sisters, brothers, and monks
48%	Necessity of having a pope
45%	Being a universal Church throughout the world
42%	Efforts toward eliminating social causes of poverty, such as unequal wages and discrimination
42%	The teaching that Christ established the authority of the bishops by choosing Peter
41%	Having a regular daily prayer life
41%	Devotion to the saints
37%	Obligation to attend Mass once a week
32%	Private confession to a priest
31%	Teachings that oppose abortion
27%	Belief that priests must be celibate
22%	Teachings that oppose the death penalty
17%	Belief that only men can be priests
14%	Church's traditional support of the right of workers to unionize

DEAN HOGE, WILLIAM DINGES, MARY JOHNSON, AND JUAN GONZALES. *YOUNG ADULT CATHOLICS*, UNIVERSITY OF NOTRE DAME PRESS, 1997, P. 201

Table 4. Boundaries of Catholic Identity

Can you be a good Catholic without this?

YES

23%	Without believing that Jesus physically rose from the dead
36%	Without believing that in the Mass, the bread and wine become the body and blood of Jesus
44%	Without donating time or money to help the poor
58%	Without obeying the Church hierarchy's teaching regarding abortion
58%	Without donating time or money to help the parish
66%	Without obeying the Church hierarchy's teaching on divorce and remarriage
67%	Without their marriage being approved by the Catholic Church
75%	Without obeying the Church hierarchy's teaching on birth control
76%	Without going to church every Sunday

"AMERICAN CATHOLICS SURVEY," *NATIONAL CATHOLIC REPORTER*, SEPTEMBER 30, 2005

Chapter Two

A Vision of Lifelong Faith Formation

As we have seen in Chapter One, the Church faces tremendous new challenges for developing a Catholic identity and Catholic way of life among all generations. In order to respond effectively and faithfully, the American Catholic Church needs to change the current paradigm of parish faith formation. In his book *Future Edge*, Joel Barker defines a paradigm this way:

> A paradigm is a set of rules and regulations (written and unwritten) that does two things: 1. it establishes or defines boundaries; and 2. it tells you how to behave inside the boundaries in order to be successful....A paradigm, in a sense, tells you that there is a game, what the game is, and how to play it successfully. The idea of a game is a very appropriate metaphor for paradigms because it reflects the need for borders and directions on how to perform correctly. A paradigm tells you how to play the game according to the rules. (p. 32, 37)

The Catholic Church is in the early stages of a major paradigm shift in faith formation. This same paradigm shift is also emerging in other Christian denominations and Judaism.[1] The new paradigm of faith formation has its roots in the earliest tradition of catechesis within the Catholic Church and has been emerging for the past forty years.

In this chapter we will examine the development of a lifelong, Church-centered paradigm of faith formation, one that holds great promise for addressing the trends in our times, and offering a hopeful vision for the future of faith formation. But first we begin with an analysis of the current paradigm of parish faith formation and why we need to change.

The Current Paradigm of Faith Formation

We are all familiar with the current or "traditional" paradigm of parish faith formation, patterned on a school model of learning. For the past fifty years, faith formation has been based on the following set of rules:

- The primary focus of faith formation is on teaching children and teens the knowledge of the faith and preparing them for sacraments: first reconciliation, first Eucharist, and confirmation.
- The participants are organized into grade levels or age groups.
- Printed texts for the participants serve as the curriculum or program.
- Courses are taught by a catechists or group leaders, usually in a classroom or a school-like setting.
- Classes are scheduled from September through May (the "school year") in sixty-minute sessions, involving approximately twenty-four sessions per year for a total of twenty-four hours of instruction.

The power of this paradigm is demonstrated in the reality that parishes all across the United States and Canada, regardless of size or region or culture, have organized faith formation in identical ways. Parishes even use these rules to organize adult education and catechumenal formation in the RCIA. It is not uncommon to find parishes offering weekly "RCIA classes" on a school-year calendar, culminating in the celebration of the sacraments of initiation at the Easter Vigil, despite the fact that the RCIA calls for comprehensive, integrated, and community-based faith formation.

The school paradigm of parish faith formation developed in a different era. It is based on a number of assumptions that no longer match the reality of our situation. Consider this: if a young person participates in classes every year for ten years from first grade through high school confirmation, he or she will participate in 240 hours, or ten days of faith formation, one day per year. We all know this is not sufficient to develop a Catholic identity and Catholic way of life. The assumption behind the school paradigm is that there is a supportive Catholic culture in the parish and home, that families are practicing their faith and that people are participating in parish life, especially Sunday Mass. As we have already seen, we can no longer assume this is true.

Over time, even the best of paradigms create more problems than they can solve. As Barker notes, "sooner or later, every paradigm begins to develop a very special set of problems that everyone in the field wants to be able to solve and no one has a clue as to how to do it" (*Future Edge*, p.

51). The longer an organization stays with the current paradigm, the more the paradigm actually strengthens the problems. This is exactly the situation in which we find ourselves today. Think for a moment about several of the most common problems in the current paradigm of faith formation.

The majority of the time, energy, and resources of the parish and staff are devoted to children, and secondarily teenagers (although with very little available for teens after confirmation or the end of high school). In many parishes over eighty percent of the parish faith formation effort is focused on only about fifteen percent of the life cycle. There is little structured, intentional faith formation for anyone before first grade or after high school. Despite document after document about the primacy of adult faith formation, is it any wonder why adult faith formation in parishes is so rare?

The primary focus on teaching individuals means that little attention is given to the family of the children or teens. Despite the importance of the family as the primary community of faith, little is being done to involve the whole family in faith formation and to empower and equip parents to nurture faith at home. The current paradigm excludes parental involvement in the faith formation of their children, and parents get the message. They learn that their primary duty is to get their sons and daughters to class on time and then pick them up on time. Most parish faith formation for children and teens is done in isolation from the family context that should reinforce and support the learning.

The emphasis on grade levels and age groups contributes to the isolation of children and teens from the rest of the parish community. In many parishes, children can progress from grade to grade and never have any meaningful contact or relationships with other generations, besides their catechist or adult leader. There are few, if any, settings for intergenerational learning and relationship-building. Is it any wonder that teenagers leave the parish after confirmation? They have never had the opportunity to develop intergenerational relationships and a sense of belonging and loyalty to the parish community. Teenagers don't leave the parish; the parish and teens were never introduced!

The structure of the textbooks used in catechetical programs is designed to repeat themes in age-appropriate ways, from childhood through adolescence. This approach divides learning into discrete, sequential, and separated units based on doctrinal themes. While texts adequately present the teachings and traditions of the Church, the content is only loosely connected to the life of the Church. Typically, the content in the textbooks does not prepare children for active participation in the life of the parish.

It is very possible that middle school teens, who are taking a course on Jesus in the Fall, could study the death and resurrection of Jesus during the Advent and Christmas season. Children study the sacraments each year, but many have no direct experience of the sacraments they are studying. Church leaders are legitimately concerned about what children and teens are being taught; however, little attention is being paid to what they are actually learning. Do children and teens have the opportunity to experience the Catholic faith they are studying? Do they have the opportunity to live and practice their faith? Are they really growing in their faith in a way that will make them lifelong learners and disciples?

The current paradigm of faith formation seems unable to involve children and teens (and their parents) in parish life, especially Sunday Mass. Even while children and teens are participating in catechetical programs, the majority do not attend Mass weekly. For far too many children, their first reconciliation and first Eucharist is their last one for a long time. Is it possible to conduct an effective catechetical program if children and teens are not participating in parish life and in the sacramental life of the Church, especially Sunday Mass?

Despite their best efforts, parishes seem unable to keep children and teens continuously engaged in catechesis from first grade through the end of high school. Participation is good during the "sacrament years"—those of first Eucharist, first reconciliation, and confirmation—but parishes struggle to provide continuity in learning and participation for the whole twelve years. It seems as long as there is sacrament preparation, people participate. But as such, the current paradigm is not producing lifelong learners; it is "graduating" teenagers after confirmation.

These problems are not new. One would think that after all these years, the current paradigm would have been able to solve these problems. Too often at meetings, workshops, and conferences, these problems are blamed on factors beyond the current faith formation paradigm, such as a lack of money, facilities, and teachers, or a lack of support from the pastor, parents, and the parish-at-large. It seems that leaders look at everything except the model of faith formation they are using.

It is very hard to acknowledge that the model of faith formation promoted by the Church and used for all these years may, in fact, be creating the problems we are experiencing. As the research in Chapter One demonstrates, the problems are getting worse. What should be obvious is that this is not a people problem, a leadership problem, a resource, money, or facility problem. It is a paradigm problem. The problems are built into the paradigm. In order to solve these problems and address the urgency of our present situation, it is time to change the paradigm.

Pioneers of the New Paradigm of Faith Formation

A new paradigm of faith formation has been emerging for the past forty years in the writing and educational work of religious education leaders. The theoretical foundations for the new paradigm can be traced through the work of C. Ellis Nelson, John Westerhoff, Berard Marthaler, Maria Harris, Charles Foster, and Catherine Dooley. Also instrumental in the growth of a new paradigm was the work of Maureen Gallagher and her colleagues on family-centered religious education in the 1980s, and the continuing work of Kathleen Chesto in family-intergenerational religious education (F.I.R.E.). In our brief survey we will see how these religious educators have contributed to the development of a new paradigm for faith formation. They are the paradigm pioneers.

C. Ellis Nelson was one of the first religious educators to critique the classroom-instructional model and emphasize that it was the community of faith that was at the heart of religious education.

> The first thing we have to do in this approach is to remove from our minds the notion that the communication of the Christian faith is directly dependent upon any instructional agencies or methods and fix in our minds the idea that faith is fostered by a community of believers, usually in a congregation. Instruction is a necessary part of the life of the congregation, but instruction must be related to the life of the congregation. (*Where Faith Begins*, p. 183)

For Nelson, "faith is communicated by a community of believers and the meaning of faith is developed by its members out of their history, by their interaction with each other, and in relation to the events that take place in their lives" (*Where Faith Begins*, p. 10).

John Westerhoff established a new foundation for religious education centered in the community of faith through a series of books beginning in the late 1960s. "Now religious education is to focus upon the communication of faith by and through a community of believers who transmit its beliefs, attitudes, and values through the myriad ways by which they live their common life together in the world." Westerhoff proposed a community of faith-inculturation paradigm in which Christian education uses every aspect of the Church's life for education.

> A viable paradigm or model for religious education needs to focus upon the radical nature of a Christian community where the tradi-

tion is faithfully transmitted through ritual and life, where persons as actors—thinking, feeling, willing, corporate selves—are nurtured and converted to radical faith, and where they are prepared and motivated for individual and corporate action in society on behalf of God's coming community. (*Will Our Children Have Faith?* p. 45)

In the new paradigm the Church has to become a significant community of faith. Westerhoff identified three aspects of community life around which we need to develop educational programs: "the rituals of the people; the experiences persons have within the community, and the actions members of the community perform, individually and corporately, in the world."

For Westerhoff, catechesis is composed of three intentional, interrelated lifelong processes: instruction (acquiring knowledge and skills), education (critical reflection on experience and the Christian faith and life in light of Scripture, tradition, and reason), and formation.

Formation is an intentional process by which culture, a people's understandings and ways of life, their world view (perceptions of reality), and their ethos (values and ways of life) are transmitted from one generation to another....Formation is best understood as the participation in and the practice of the Christian life of faith. It is a process of transformation and formation, of conversion and nurture. It is a natural process that is intentional. (*Will Our Children Have Faith?* p. 139, 140)

All three are essential, but only formation is normative; education and instruction are contributive.

Berard Marthaler developed a socialization model of faith formation that describes how the community of faith transmits its culture from generation to generation. Culture is the

explicit and implicit values and patterns of meaning embodied in configurations of behavior, social institutions, and all the traits and artifacts that give a particular group its distinctive identity. They are the symbols that constitute and give expression to a culture. Thus culture is understood as a comprehensive symbol system that gives meaning and value to every aspect of social living. ("Socialization as Model for Catechetics," *Foundations of Religious Education*, p. 68)

Socialization happens in the interplay between the individual and the community which is transmitting the culture, or in the case of Catholicism, the symbols, beliefs, values, and practices of the Catholic faith and the Catholic way of life. Through socialization within a community of faith, the individual develops a Catholic identity.

Catechesis, or faith formation as socializing, embodies the threefold goal

> that has concerned the Christian community from New Testament times: 1. the broadening of one's horizons—growth in personal faith, 2. the gradual incorporation of members into a society of believers—religious belonging, and 3. the maintenance and transmission of a particular symbol system that constitutes and express Catholic identity—communicating meaning. ("Socialization as Model for Catechetics," p. 88)

Marthaler identifies several of the strengths of the socialization model:

1. The socialization model opens the way for a stronger emphasis in religious education on process. This is not to say that methodology assumes the chief role, but rather it is an honest acknowledgement that catechesis in the final analysis is community education. The community of faith with all its formal and informal structures is the chief catechist. Professionals and paraprofessionals engaged in various aspects of educational ministry are its agents.

2. Catechesis is not merely with individuals but with the community taken as a whole. The socialization process implies the transformation as well as transmission of culture. Just as the individual Christian needs to undergo continuous conversion, so, too, must the Christian community constantly broaden its horizons, reforming and renewing itself. Catechists thus become agents of change.

3. The content of religious education is not "faith" as a kind of abstraction. It is always mediated by a symbol system. The teaching of doctrine becomes a means—albeit one of the most important—in communicating meaning and giving the community a sense of identity. Religious language—myths, parables, and other narratives—and theology are other means of transmitting the symbols of faith. The success or failure of catechetical programs must be ultimately judged in terms of how effectively the socialization process is proceeding, not in terms of how much information church members have. ("Socialization as Model for Catechetics," p. 89).

In *Fashion Me a People*, Maria Harris provides the clearest image of the "ancient-new" paradigm of faith formation in this ecclesial model of faith formation in which the Church's educational ministry is embodied and lived in five classical forms: *koinonia*, *leiturgia*, *kerygma*, *diakonia*, and *didache*. The Church educates to all of these five classical forms, as well as *through* all of them:

- to *koinonia* (community and communion) by engaging in the forms of community and communion;
- to *leiturgia* (worship and prayer) by engaging in the forms of prayer and worship and spirituality;
- to *kerygma* (proclaiming the word of God) by attention to, practicing, and incarnating the kerygma, "Jesus is risen," in the speech of our own lives, especially the speech of advocacy;
- to *diakonia* (service and outreach) by attention to our own service and reaching out to others, personally and communally, locally and globally;
- to *didache* (teaching and learning) by attention to the most appropriate forms of teaching and learning (including schooling in our own communities).

Should any of these be left out as full partners in the educational work of ministry, should any of these be downplayed, should any of these be exalted to the denigration of others, we would not be able to educate fully. All are needed. (*Fashion Me a People*, p. 43-44)

In this ecclesial model, the whole Church, through its five forms, is the curriculum. When the Church is viewed as the curriculum it becomes clear that the Church does not have an educational program; it is an educational program.

The five classical forms provide a setting for learning that goes beyond instruction and the classroom model, and provides a faith community context for learning. Harris writes,

The heritage of Scripture, tradition, the lives of our ancestors in the faith, creed, gospel, prayer, sacrament, and law is often taught better through worship or preaching than through classroom instruction. The tradition itself is handed on more fully when it is done in the midst of the people, the community, who are the tradition in their own persons. The life of prayer educates us most not when we read books about it but when we fall on our knees. The sacramental life nourishes us when we take part in baptizing, in confirming, and in coming together to the table. (*Fashion Me a People*, p. 44)

Each of these five classical forms are interdependent.

When we say the words of justice and do the work of justice, our speaking and doing are credible only if outreach and service are associated with the more inner-directed works of teaching, learning, and prayer. At the same time, outreach and service combined with prayer and study—with leiturgia and didache—ensure that the work of justice will be informed and careful, based on solid thought, serious scholarship, and intelligent probing. They can make us strong in the head as well as in the heart. (*Fashion Me a People*, p. 45)

In this ecclesial framework the whole community is educating and empowering the whole community to engage in ministry in the midst of the world. The congregation is becoming a community of learning and practice.

> The whole community as agent is, by its way of living together, speaking together, praying together, and worshiping together, causing a shock of recognition in person after person that reveals them to themselves, saying, "I am being educated by and in this community to become who I am."…The whole community is coming to know itself as learner, to know itself as the subject of education, and to know itself as the one whose path is unending. (*Fashion Me a People*, p. 49)

Harris proposed a comprehensive, integrated, and Church-centered model of faith formation that is guiding the new paradigm today. The vision and themes of her work strongly resonate with the *General Directory for Catechesis* which presents a comprehensive, ecclesial model of catechesis. (The next section will present the new paradigm themes in the GDC.)

Charles Foster pioneered an understanding of the faith community as the primary educator and proposed the events of Church life as the foundation of a lifelong faith formation curriculum.

> The gospel originated in acts of God experienced as events by communities of people. Something happened long ago in the life, death, and resurrection of Jesus Christ that transformed perspectives, commitments, and ways of living among a small band of people in a small Mediterranean country. The stories of that event have gathered people into its possibilities for centuries, shaping and transforming their lives and culminating in communities of memory and transformation. (*Educating Congregations*, p. 38)

For Foster, the life of the Church is centered in events that have the power to educate and transform individuals and the community. As Catholics, these include Church year feasts and seasons, sacraments and liturgy, justice and service, prayer and spiritual traditions, community life. But if these events are to become important to people, people must be familiar with them. If we want people to participate in these events and be transformed by them, we must help people understand these events and learn *how* to participate in them. Over time people begin to identify with the events and take on their character.

We discover ourselves in a community of people identified with that event. We begin to see the world through the perspective of the community originating in and shaped by that event....These events not only tell us who we are, but also to whom we belong. They provide us with clues about how we are to relate to others and to participate in the world around us. (*Educating Congregations*, p. 38)

There are four kinds of events that shape the life and mission of the faith community. These events become the basis of a church's curriculum and the focus of parish learning programs and household faith formation.

- *Paradigmatic events*. The patterns for Christian life and community have their origin in significant events deeply rooted in our tradition. The central paradigmatic event or pattern is the life, death, and resurrection of Jesus Christ: the paschal mystery. This event establishes the framework for the Church year and the liturgical life of the parish. Paradigmatic events provide a persistent structure that gives order and purpose to our common lives.

- *Seasonal events*. Our participation in the narrative structure of paradigmatic events occurs through a series of seasonal events that gather us up into repeated activities of telling and retelling, interpreting and re-interpreting, embodying and re-enacting the stories associated with them. The Church year feasts and seasons help to provide a rhythmic pattern for the life of the parish. The ritual processes that structure these events carry the Church through the liturgical seasons from Advent through Christmas, Epiphany, Lent, Easter, Pentecost, through the calendar of saints' days, and through local seasons and ethnic traditions. Whether liturgical or nonliturgical, seasonal events order and move the life of the community through the year. Everyone participates; everyone benefits. These events provide the clearest and most consistent structure for the education of a parish community.

- *Occasional events*. Occasional events intensify community identity and mission, illuminate community meanings, and energize community life. These events, such as the celebration of a baptism, a wedding, a funeral, a church dedication, or a special mission project, provide occasions for telling other kinds of stories integral to the paradigmatic gospel story that gives the parish its reason for being. These events include the celebration of the sacraments (Eucharist, baptism, reconciliation, confirmation, marriage, anointing of the sick, holy orders), funerals, commissionings, birthdays, and anniversaries. They also include actions of justice and service, and community life events. The participation of people in these events is heightened and the significance of these events is enhanced when people prepare to participate in them.

- *Spontaneous events.* These events surprise the faith community with unexpected opportunities to rehearse and renew its participation in the meaning of ancient events and their stories. These events bring joy and sorrow, blessing and suffering. Spontaneous events come in many forms: a changing population in the parish or neighborhood, the loss of a pastor, the destruction of the church building by fire, or the construction of a church building, among many other possibilities.

Catherine Dooley has pioneered principles and approaches for liturgical/sacramental catechesis that can be expanded and applied to the new paradigm of faith formation that takes the faith community as its starting point for catechesis. The purpose of liturgical catechesis is to

> lead communities and individual members of the faithful to maturity of faith through full and active participation in the liturgy, which affects and expresses that faith in the conscious living-out of a life of justice and...to enable believers to come to a full, conscious, and active participation that expresses and deepens relationships: relationship to God and to one another in Christ through the Spirit. ("Liturgical Catechesis for Confirmation," *Traditions and Transitions*, p. 255)

In her descriptions of the purposes of liturgical catechesis we can see an application to all faith formation: catechesis directed toward leading communities and individual members of the faithful to maturity through full and active participation in the life of the Church, which includes liturgy and sacraments, prayer, justice and service, and Church year feasts and seasons.

In the new paradigm, the principles of liturgical/sacramental catechesis are expanded to apply to all faith formation.

- *Principle: The rite itself—the word of God, the symbols, the symbolic actions, and the prayer texts—is the center of the catechesis.* In the new paradigm the Church event is the center of catechesis. We find embedded in each event the content—the beliefs and practices—of the Catholic faith. The content emerges from the event itself, just as it does from the rite.
- *Principle: The word of God is integral to the liturgical celebration.* In the new paradigm the word of God is integral to and experienced

in each Church event. Learning programs to prepare the community for the Church event incorporate study of the appropriate Scripture readings, for example: the lectionary readings for the season or feast, the Scripture readings in a sacramental ritual, the scriptural foundation of Catholic social teaching, Scripture teachings of morality, and praying with the Scriptures.

- *Principle: In liturgical/sacramental catechesis symbols and symbolic actions are the language of faith.*

  > Symbols and symbolic actions are the ways in which the presence of Christ and his mystery is manifest to the worshipping community and the way in which the community's response to God's initiative is made evident. The liturgical action, which revolves around the central symbols of gathering the assembly, proclaiming of the word, immersing in water, sharing of the bread and wine, anointing with oil, laying on of hands, aims to enable the people of God to experience the mystery of God and to lead lives of Christian discipleship. ("Mystagogy: A Model for Sacramental Catechesis," *The Candles Are Still Burning*, p. 61)

In the new paradigm, all of the events of Church life are explored so that through the symbols, the actions, and the traditions of each event the presence of Christ and his mystery can be experienced and people can be transformed.

- *Principle: "The assembly has a right and an obligation to full, active and conscious participation in the liturgy"* ("Mystagogy: A Model for Sacramental Catechesis," p. 61). In the new paradigm, catechesis prepares the community for "full, active, and conscious participation" in Church life, and in so doing, helps the community to assume its responsibility for sharing faith with each other.

- *Principle: Catechesis is an integrated process of formation.*

  > Catechesis includes building up the community, integrating scriptural and doctrinal instruction into reflection on experience, leading to private and liturgical prayer and motivating the acts of justice. Catechesis is an ongoing process, and an awareness of the formative nature of ritual is a constitutive element of that process. The *Catechism of the Catholic Church* states that the liturgy is "the privileged place for catechizing the People of God" (#1074) and calls for a liturgical catechesis, which "aims to initiative people into the mystery of Christ by proceeding from the visible to the invisible, from the sign to the thing signified, from the 'sacraments' to

the 'mysteries' (#1075)." ("Mystagogy: A Model for Sacramental Catechesis," p. 62)

In the new paradigm, catechesis as an integrated process of formation is the guiding image for all faith formation in the parish community.

- *Principle: The liturgical year expresses and shapes Christian identity.*

> In the course of the year the whole mystery of Christ is recalled and the culmination of the Church year is the Easter Triduum of the passion and resurrection of Christ. All of the Sundays, seasons, and feasts of the year express a different aspect of the paschal mystery. The penitential and baptismal character of Lent, the vigilance and expectation of Advent, the beginning of the paschal mystery manifested in the birth, epiphany, and baptism of Jesus in the Christmas season, and accounts of Jesus' ministry and the celebration of the paschal mystery in all of its aspects in Ordinary Time shape and express Catholic identity as well as promoting formation and participation in the life of the Church. ("Mystagogy: A Model for Sacramental Catechesis," p. 62)

In the new paradigm, the Church year is the heart of faith formation for the parish community, providing the structure for the events of Church life as well as the lifelong curriculum.

Summary of Key Insights

From this very brief survey of six pioneers we can see the outlines of a new paradigm of lifelong, ecclesial faith formation for the whole parish community. The major lessons we learn from C. Ellis Nelson, John Westerhoff, Berard Marthaler, Maria Harris, Charles Foster, and Catherine Dooley are:

- The Church community is the primary communicator of the faith tradition and practices.
- The entire life of the Church is the curriculum and primary teacher through its five classical forms: didache, koinonia, kerygma, diakonia, and leiturgia. The Church itself is the "educational program."
- The parish and home are called to be faith communities of learning and practice. The whole community is both learner and teacher.
- Faith formation is an integrated process incorporating
    1. formation through participation in the life of the faith community,
    2. education in Scripture and the Catholic tradition,
    3. apprenticeship in the Christian life,

4. intimate connection with the liturgy and rituals of the Church,
5. development of a life of prayer, and
6. engagement in actions of justice and service.

- Faith formation is a process of transformation (conversion) and formation (nurture). It is participation in and the practice of the Catholic way of life.

- The events of the parish community—Church year feasts and seasons, sacraments and liturgy, justice and service, prayer and spiritual traditions, and community life—have the power to educate and transform individuals, families, and the entire community. Faith formation prepares people for meaningful participation in the life of the Church.

- The content of event-centered faith formation comes from the life of the Church and the event itself. The content emerges from the event itself.

Each of these pioneers has added important insights and elements to the new paradigm of lifelong faith formation.

The Pioneering Vision of the *General Directory for Catechesis*

The best presentation of the Church's catechetical vision is found in the 1997 *General Directory for Catechesis*, which both integrates the developing vision since the publication of the 1971 edition and provides a foundation for the continued growth of catechesis in the Catholic Church. The *General Directory for Catechesis* provides the "fundamental theologico-pastoral principles drawn from the Church's Magisterium, particularly those inspired by the Second Vatican Council, which are capable of better orienting and coordinating the pastoral activity of the ministry of the word, and, concretely, catechesis" (cf. *General Catechetical Directory* [DCG], [1971], Introduction) (GDC #9).

Embedded within the theologico-pastoral principles of the *General Directory for Catechesis* and the *National Directory for Catechesis* (2005) are foundational themes for a new paradigm of faith formation.

Theme 1. Discipleship and Continuing Conversion

The *General Directory for Catechesis* sets forth a challenging goal for all faith formation: "to encourage a living, explicit and fruitful profession of faith" (GDC #66) and to "put people not only in touch, but also in communion and intimacy, with Jesus Christ" (GDC #80). The *National*

Directory for Catechesis states it this way: "The object of catechesis is communion with Jesus Christ. Catechesis leads people to enter the mystery of Christ, to encounter him, and to discover themselves and the meaning of their lives in him" (NDC 19B, p. 55).

Catechesis empowers people of all ages and generations to live as disciples of Jesus Christ and active members of the Catholic community. It focuses on continuing conversion to Jesus Christ and a life of committed discipleship. "Faith is a gift destined to grow in the hearts of believers (*Catechesi Tradendae* [CT], 20a: "It is in fact a matter of giving growth, at the level of knowledge and in life, to the seed of faith sown by the Holy Spirit with the initial proclamation."). Adhering to Jesus Christ, in fact, sets in motion a process of continuing conversion, which lasts for the whole of life" (cf. *Redemptoris Missio* [RM], 46b) (GDC #56).

Theme 2. A Church of Living Signs

At the center of all catechesis is the Church. The *General Directory for Catechesis* envisions a Church of living signs, a community which is "living catechesis." In fact, living signs is the core catechetical message of the GDC. This is exactly the way Jesus spoke to the disciples of John the Baptist when they asked him if he was the promised one: "And he answered them, 'Go and tell John what you have seen and heard: the blind receive their sight, the lame walk, the lepers are cleansed, the deaf hear, the dead are raised, the poor have good news brought to them'" (Luke 7:22).

Michael Warren reflects on the theology of Church found in the *General Directory for Catechesis* when he writes,

> The 1997 GDC highlights the local Church as the sacrament of the encounter with the living Spirit of Jesus, the Christian reality at its most primary level. If Jesus is the sacrament of the human encounter with God, then the Church is the sacrament of the human encounter with the living Spirit of Jesus. This means that the "agent of catechesis" is not any individual catechist. The agent of catechesis is "the Church animated by the Holy Spirit" (GDC #77). Catechesis is an essentially ecclesial act, and when the local corporate body of believers is in fact the Church animated by the Holy Spirit, it becomes the main "agent" of catechesis proclaiming the Gospel (cf. GDC #78): the Christian community is in herself living catechesis.... (GDC #141)
>
> This insight, a unifying theme of the revised *Directory*, suggests that parish catechetical directors and the catechists working with them cannot understand their own efforts without seeing them as directed to the witness of the life of the local Church. Their task is

fostering the gospel life of the ecclesial body itself. The local Church's enfleshing of the gospel is the master communicator of the gospel; and lacking that witness, the efforts of the individual catechist have little effect. What else does the following passage mean? "Catechesis is nothing other than the process of transmitting the Gospel, as the Christian community has received it, understands it, celebrates it, lives it and communicates it in many ways" (GDC #105). ("A New Priority in Pastoral Ministry," *Living Light*, p. 8)

The life of the parish community itself constitutes the fundamental experience of catechesis: "the parish is, without doubt, the most important *locus* in which the Christian community is formed and expressed" (GDC #257).

The parish is where the Church lives. Parishes are communities of action, and of hope. They are where the gospel is proclaimed and celebrated, where believers are formed and sent to renew the earth. Parishes are the home of the Christian community; they are the heart of our Church. Parishes are the place where God's people meet Jesus in word and sacrament and come in touch with the source of the Church's life. (USCCB, *Communities of Salt and Light*, p. 1)

As is so evident in the work of Maria Harris, John Westerhoff, and the other paradigm pioneers, faith is communicated through the Christian community. The new paradigm takes the Church of living signs as its starting point for lifelong catechesis. This insight reshapes everything about catechesis including the curriculum and learning process.

Theme 3. The Church as a Source, Locus, and Means of Catechesis

Catechesis "is an essentially ecclesial act—an action of the Church" and as such the Church is "the origin, *locus*, and means of catechesis." Catechesis is a responsibility of the entire Christian community. The *General Directory for Catechesis* makes it clear that the Church is the curriculum and the primary teacher.

Catechetical pedagogy will be effective to the extent that the Christian community becomes a point of concrete reference for the faith journey of individuals. This happens when the community is proposed as a source, *locus* and means of catechesis. Concretely, the community becomes a visible place of faith-witness. It provides for the formation of its members. It receives them as the family of God. It constitutes itself as the living and permanent environment for growth in faith (cf. *Ad Gentes* 14; DCG 35; CT 24). (GDC #158)

The *National Directory for Catechesis* describes the Church as the natural environment for catechesis. She provides the primary setting for the proclamation of the Gospel, the point of welcome for those who seek to know the Lord, the place where men and women are invited to conversion and discipleship, the environment for the celebration of the sacraments, and the motivation for apostolic witness in the world. (NDC 19C, p. 57)

In the new paradigm, the whole life of the Church is its faith curriculum. Everything about it makes it a teaching and learning community. By focusing on Scripture, tradition, and the events of the parish community (liturgy, sacraments, justice and service, Church year feasts and seasons, prayer and devotions, community activities), lifelong catechesis provides a curriculum for the whole parish community. The fundamental unity of the parish is strengthened by establishing this common focus for catechesis that engages all members of the community in learning at home and in the parish. Catechesis creates a culture of learning in which learning permeates every aspect of the parish community.

Theme 4. Twin Tasks: Permanent Catechesis and Catechesis for the New Evangelization

The GDC and NDC both situate catechesis within the evangelizing activity of the Church. Within this context catechesis has two tasks: to provide a permanent or ongoing catechesis that sustains and nurtures conversion in those with mature faith (see GDC #69), and a "second catechesis" to those who were baptized but were never effectively evangelized or catechized (see NDC 17A). Permanent or ongoing catechesis "involves the systematic presentation of the truths of the faith and the practice of Christian living. The function of permanent catechesis is to nourish the faith of believers through their lives" (NDC 17C).

Catechesis for the new evangelization recognizes the large number of baptized Catholics

who were never effectively evangelized before, to those who have never made a personal commitment to Christ and the Gospel, to those formed by the values of the secularized culture, to those who have lost a sense of faith, and to those who are alienated....The new evangelization is aimed at personal transformation through the development of a personal relationship with God, participation in sacramental worship, the development of a mature ethical and social conscience, ongoing catechesis, and a deepening integration of faith into all areas of life. (NDC 17A, p. 47)

A catechesis centered in the events of Church life and in participation in the parish community deepens and sustains the faith of believers and re-introduces those who have never made a faith commitment to Jesus Christ to him, his gospel, and the Catholic tradition.

Theme 5. Six Fundamental Tasks

The GDC and NDC present six essential and interdependent tasks for catechesis:

1. knowledge of the faith,
2. knowledge of the meaning of liturgy and the sacraments,
3. moral formation in Jesus Christ,
4. teaching how to pray with Christ,
5. preparing to live in community and participate actively in the life and mission of the Church, and
6. a missionary spirit that prepares the faithful to be present as Christians in society (see GDC #85-87 and NDC 20, pp. 60-63).

"These six tasks constitute a unified whole by which catechesis seeks to achieve its objective: the formation of disciples of Jesus Christ" (NDC 20, p. 63). This comprehensive formation is rooted in Christ's method of formation:

> Jesus instructed his disciples; he prayed with them; he showed them how to live; and he gave them his mission. Christ's method of formation was accomplished by diverse yet interrelated tasks. His example is the most fruitful inspiration for effective catechesis today because it is integral to formation in the Christian faith. Catechesis must attend to each of these different dimensions of faith; each becomes a distinct yet complementary task. Faith must be known, celebrated, lived, and expressed in faith. So catechesis comprises six fundamental tasks, each of which is related to an aspect of faith in Christ. All efforts in evangelization and catechesis should incorporate these tasks. (NDC 20, p. 59-60)

This is a comprehensive and robust vision of catechesis. Each task is necessary so that the Christian faith can attain full development. A lifelong curriculum, centered in the life and events of Church life, naturally incorporates all six tasks of catechesis. One can hear in the vision of the GDC and NDC a strong resonance with the five classical forms of Church life and their interrelationships as described by Maria Harris, and in the RCIA's vision of catechumenal formation, to which we now turn.

Theme 6. The Catechumenate as a Model of Catechizing Activity

The *General Directory for Catechesis* envisions the baptismal catechumenate as a model of catechizing activity with its integrated catechesis incorporating

1. formation through participation in the life of the faith community,

2. education in Scripture and the Catholic tradition,

3. apprenticeship in the Christian life,

4. intimate connection with the liturgy and rituals of the Church,

5. development of a life of prayer, and

6. engagement in actions of justice and service (see GDC #90).

The baptismal catechumenate also provides a learning process for all catechesis:

1. preparation for discipleship and full, conscious, and active participation in Church life;

2. experience of Church life—the encounter with Jesus Christ, the Scriptures and the tradition—through Sunday liturgy, the sacraments, Church year feasts and seasons, justice and service, prayer and devotions, and eventually through the celebration of the sacraments of initiation; and finally,

3. reflection on the significance and meaning of learning and application to living as a disciple at home and in the world (mystagogy).

Theme 7. The "Church of the Home" as a Unique Locus for Catechesis

The *General Directory for Catechesis* recognizes the family as the "church of the home" or "domestic church" and a unique locus for catechesis.

> ...in every Christian family the different aspects and functions of the life of the entire Church may be reflected: mission; catechesis; witness; prayer etc. Indeed in the same way as the Church, the family "is a place in which the Gospel is transmitted and from which it extends." (cf. *Evangelii Nuntiandi* [EN] 71) The family as a *locus* of catechesis has a unique privilege: transmitting the Gospel by rooting it in the context of profound human values. (cf. *Gaudium et Spes* [GS] 52; *Familaris Consortio* [FC] 37a)...It is, indeed, a Christian education more witnessed to than taught, more occasional than systematic, more ongoing and daily than structured into periods. (GDC #255)

This vision of the family is reinforced by the *National Directory for Catechesis*:

The Christian family is ordinarily the first experience of the Christian community and the primary environment for growth in faith. Because it is the "church of the home" (FC 38), the family provides a unique *locus* for catechesis. It is a place in which the word of God is received and from which it is extended. Within the Christian family, parents are the primary educators in the faith and "the first heralds of the faith with regard to their children" (*Lumen Gentium* [LG] 11). But all the members make up the family, and each can make a unique contribution to creating the basic environment in which a sense of God's loving presence is awakened and faith in Jesus Christ is confessed, encouraged, and lived. (NDC 29D, pp. 100-101)

At every stage of the life cycle and in its different faces and structures, the family is at the very heart of the new paradigm. No longer an add-on to the work of faith formation, the family and home is now central to all faith formation efforts.

First, the new paradigm promotes faith sharing and practice at home by engaging households in lifelong catechesis as a family or household, providing opportunities to learn together and develop the knowledge and skills for sharing faith, celebrating traditions, and practicing the Catholic faith. Second, families and households are empowered and equipped to build faith-filled communities at home: integrating the Catholic faith and values into the fabric of home life, sharing faith around Scripture and the Catholic tradition, praying together and celebrating rituals as part of the pattern of daily and seasonal home life, caring for each other and those in their community, and working for justice and serving those in need locally and globally.

Theme 8. Faith and Culture

The inculturation of the gospel "involves listening to the culture of the people for an echo of the word of God. It involves the discernment of the presence of authentic Gospel values or openness to authentic Gospel values in the culture" (NDC 21C, p. 64). Inculturation correlates faith and life. In a multicultural and pluralistic society,

It seeks to open the hearts and minds of people to "receive Jesus Christ in every dimension of their life. The process of inculturation must involve the people to whom the Gospel is addressed, so that they can receive the faith and reflect it" (NDC 21C, p. 65).

Catechesis inculturates the gospel message so that it is proclaimed and taught in the language and culture of the people. A catechesis of inculturation means presenting the teaching of the faith in a complete and authentic way in dialogue with the language, customs, and practices of those to whom the gospel is presented (see also GDC #109-113, 203).

The *National Directory for Catechesis* identifies several catechetical tasks essential to the inculturation of faith:

- To discover the seeds of the Gospel that may be present in the culture
- To know and respect the essential elements and basic expressions of the culture of the persons to whom it is addressed
- To recognize that the Gospel message is both transcendent and immanent—it is not bound by the limitations of any single human culture, yet it has a cultural dimension, that in which Jesus of Nazareth lived
- To proclaim the transforming and regenerating force that the Gospel works in every culture
- To promote a new enthusiasm for the Gospel in accordance with evangelized culture
- To use the language and culture of the people as a foundation to express the common faith of the Church
- To maintain the integral content of faith and avoid obscuring the content of the Christian message by adaptations that would compromise or diminish the deposit of faith. (NDC 21C, p. 65)

The tasks set out by the NDC provide specific direction for a catechesis that takes inculturation seriously. The new paradigm seeks to inculturate the gospel message in the ethnic cultures of the Catholic Church. When the curriculum is centered on the life and events of the Church, the parish can incorporate the cultural traditions of the community into both the lifelong curriculum and household practice. When the learning process utilizes the language and cultural experiences of the community, the gospel can more effectively form and transform people of all ages.

The new paradigm also seeks to inculturate catechesis in the postmodern culture of contemporary society. When faith formation incorporates the characteristics of the culture—experiential, participative, interactive, image-driven, and connected—in both the content of catechesis and the style of learning, the gospel message can more effectively form and transform people. When faith formation takes seriously the challenge of re-traditioning, it can rediscover the events and traditions of Catholicism and incorporate them in the curriculum so that they can reshape contemporary life.

Summary of Key Insights

The *General Directory for Catechesis* and the *National Directory for Catechesis* provide foundational themes to guide the development of the new paradigm of faith formation:

- Continuing conversion and a life of committed discipleship.
- A Church of living signs which is living catechesis for all its members.
- The whole life of the Church as the faith formation curriculum.
- A systematic lifelong curriculum that provides foundational catechesis throughout life.
- An evangelizing catechesis providing both permanent catechesis and "a second catechesis."
- A comprehensive catechesis of six tasks constituting a unified whole.
- An integrated catechesis embodying the elements of the baptismal catechumenate.
- The family as the "Church of the home" and a unique *locus* for catechesis.
- A catechesis that inculturates the gospel in the ethnic cultures of the Catholic Church and within the postmodern culture of contemporary society.

A New Paradigm: Lifelong, Church-Centered Faith Formation

The new paradigm of lifelong, Church-centered ecclesial faith formation incorporates both a vision and a set of practices to give shape and form to the vision. The vision for this new paradigm of lifelong faith formation has developed from the work of religious educators and the catechetical vision of the Catholic Church as presented in the *General Directory for Catechesis* and the *National Directory for Catechesis*.

The vision of lifelong, Church-centered faith formation has the following characteristics:

- To nurture the Catholic identity of all parishioners for a lifetime.
- To utilize the whole life of the Church as its faith formation curriculum: Church year feasts and seasons, sacraments and liturgy, justice and service, prayer and spirituality, community life.
- To re-engage all generations in participating in Catholic community life, especially Sunday Mass.

- To involve all generations in learning together through intergenerational learning.
- To equip and support families, and especially parents, to create a pattern of family faith sharing and a Catholic way of life.
- To address the hungers of the post-Vatican II generations of Catholics for experience, participation, interaction, connection and community, spirituality and meaning, and practices for living.
- To transform the parish community into a community of lifelong learners, engaging everyone as both teacher and learner.

The lifelong faith formation paradigm is not a new program. Programs are specific ways to implement a vision. They are *not* the vision! Lifelong faith formation is a fundamentally new way of doing faith formation that supplants the schooling, classroom paradigm of faith formation. The new paradigm has a distinct vision and set of practices to implement the vision. It is a complete system of lifelong faith formation for all generations that creates a community of learning and practice at home and in the parish. It creates a culture of learning and practice, so that faith growth and learning permeate every aspect of the parish and home.

A new vision requires a new set of practices. Without a set of new practices for faith formation there will be a gap between vision and reality. How often have you taken a course or workshop that inspires you with a new vision for faith formation or parish life? How many workshops have you attended on the primacy of adult faith formation or the importance of nurturing family faith? You are inspired and want to apply your new insights, but you confront the reality of the old paradigm. Lacking the specific practices to bring the vision to reality, you return to the old ways of doing things and occasionally implement a new idea that you received at the course or workshop.

Practices bring the vision to life. The practices of lifelong faith formation give shape and form to the vision so that it can be tailored to the unique culture and character of a parish community. There are four essential practices for lifelong faith formation. The application of these practices will turn the vision into reality in a parish setting:

Practice 1. Events-centered curriculum for the whole parish community

Practice 2. Events-centered intergenerational learning for all generations

Practice 3. Household faith formation

Practice 4. Collaborative and empowering leadership.

Research and pastoral experience have demonstrated that it takes all four practices, working together, to effectively implement lifelong faith formation. The four practices are interdependent; they support each other. Chapters Three through Six will present the key practices for turning the vision of the new paradigm into reality.

End Notes

1. For resources on the emerging trend read: *Becoming a Congregation of Learners: Learning as a Key to Revitalizing Congregational Life* by Isa Aron (Woodstock, VT: Jewish Lights Publishing, 2001), and *A Congregation of Learners: Transforming the Synagogue into a Learning Community* edited by Isa Aron, Sara Lee, and Seymour Rosse. (New York: UAHC Press, 1995).

Works Cited

Barker, Joel. **Future Edge: Discovering the New Paradigms of Success**. New York: William Morrow, 1992.

Congregation for the Clergy. **General Directory for Catechesis**. Washington, DC: USCCB Publishing, 1997.

Dooley, Catherine. "Mystagogy: A Model for Sacramental Catechesis," **The Candles Are Still Burning**. Edited by Mary Grey, Andree Heaton, and Danny Sullivan. Collegeville, MN: Liturgical Press, 1995.

— — —. "Liturgical Catechesis for Confirmation," **Traditions and Transitions**. Edited by Eleanor Bernstein, CSJ and Martin Connell. Chicago: LTP, 1998.

Foster, Charles. **Educating Congregations**. Nashville: Abingdon, 1994.

Harris, Maria. **Fashion Me a People: Curriculum in the Church**. Louisville, KY: Westminister/John Knox Press, 1989.

Marthaler, Berard. "Socialization as Model for Catechetics," **Foundations of Religious Education**. Edited by Michael Warren. Winona, MN: St. Mary's Press, 1997.

Nelson, C. Ellis. **Where Faith Begins**. Richmond, VA: John Knox Press, 1967.

United States Conference of Catholic Bishops. **National Directory for Catechesis**. Washington, DC: USCCB Publishing, 2005.

— — —. **Communities of Salt and Light**. Washington, DC: USCCB, 1993.

Warren, Michael. "A New Priority in Pastoral Ministry," **Living Light** Volume 37, Number 1 (Fall 2000).

Westerhoff, John. **Will Our Children Have Faith?** (revised edition). New York: Morehouse Publishing, 2000.

For Further Reading

Aron, Isa. **Becoming a Congregation of Learners: Learning as a Key to Revitalizing Congregational Life**. Woodstock, VT: Jewish Lights Publishing, 2001.

Aron, Isa, Sara Lee, and Seymour Rossel. **A Congregation of Learners: Transforming the Synagogue into a Learning Community**. New York: UAHC Press, 1995.

Darcy-Berube, Francoise. **Religious Education at the Crossroads**. New York: Paulist Press, 1995.

Dooley, Catherine. "Renewing the Parish," **Living Light** Volume 40, Number 1 (Fall 2003).

———. "Liturgical Catechesis for Confirmation," **Traditions and Transitions**. Edited by Eleanor Bernstein, CSJ and Martin Connell. Chicago: LTP, 1998.

———. "From the Visible to the Invisible: Mystagogy in the Catechism of the Catholic Church," **Living Light** (Spring 1995).

———. "Mystagogy: A Model for Sacramental Catechesis," **The Candles Are Still Burning**. Edited by Mary Grey, Andree Heaton, and Danny Sullivan. Collegeville, MN: Liturgical Press, 1995.

———. "Catechumenate for Children: Sharing the Gift of Faith," **Readings in the Christian Initiation of Children**. Edited by Victoria Tufano. Chicago: LTP, 1994.

———. "Baptismal Catechesis for Children of Catechetical Age," **Issues in the Christian Initiation of Children**. Edited by Kathy Brown and Frank Sokol. Chicago: LTP, 1989.

———. "The Lectionary as a Sourcebook for Catechesis in the Catechumenate," **Before and After Baptism**. Edited by James Wilde. Chicago: LTP, 1988.

Dykstra, Craig. **Growing in the Life of Faith: Education and Christian Practices**. Louisville, KY: Geneva Press, 1998.

Foster, Charles and Theodore Brelsford. **We Are the Church Together: Cultural Diversity in Congregational Life**. Valley Forge, PA: Trinity Press International, 1996.

Foster, Charles. **Embracing Diversity**. Washington, DC: Alban Institute, 1997.

———. **Educating Congregations**. Nashville: Abingdon, 1994.

———. **Teaching in the Community of Faith**. Nashville: Abingdon Press, 1982.

— — —. "The Faith Community as a Guiding Image for Christian Education." **Contemporary Approaches to Christian Education**. Edited by Jack L. Seymour and Donald E. Miller. Nashville: Abingdon Press, 1982.

— — —. "Intergenerational Religious Education," **Changing Patterns of Religious Education**. Edited by Marvin Taylor. Nashville: Abingdon Press, 1984.

Groome, Thomas and Michael J. Corso, editors. **Empowering Catechetical Leaders**. Washington, DC: National Catholic Education Association, 1999.

Harris, Maria. **Fashion Me a People: Curriculum in the Church**. Louisville, KY: Westminister/John Knox Press, 1989.

Mongoven, Anne Marie. **The Prophetic Spirit of Catechesis**. New York: Paulist Press, 2000.

Nelson, C. Ellis. **Where Faith Begins**. Richmond, VA: John Knox Press, 1967.

Pope John Paul II. **Catechesis Tradendae**. Washington, DC: USCC Publishing, 1979.

Regan, Jane. **Toward an Adult Church: A Vision of Faith Formation**. Chicago: Loyola Press, 2002.

Westerhoff, John. **Will Our Children Have Faith?** (revised edition). New York: Morehouse Publishing, 2000.

— — —. **Living the Faith Community: The Church that Makes a Difference**. San Francisco: Harper & Row, 1985.

Westerhoff, John and William Willimon. **Liturgy and Learning through the Life Cycle**. (Revised Edition) Akron, OH: OSL Publications, 1980, 1994.

Westerhoff, John and Gwen Kennedy Neville. **Learning through Liturgy**. New York: Seabury Press, 1978.

— — —. Neville. **Generation to Generation**. Philadelphia: United Church Press, 1974.

Westerhoff, John, editor. **A Colloquy on Christian Education**. Philadelphia: United Church Press, 1972.

Chapter Three

Practices of Lifelong Faith Formation

An Events-Centered Systematic Curriculum for All Generations

Events-Centered Faith Formation

At the heart of the lifelong faith formation paradigm are the events of Church life. The lifelong curriculum and learning programs are fashioned around the events of our shared life as Church: Church year feasts and seasons, sacraments and liturgy, prayer traditions and spiritual practices, justice and service, and community life. The *General Directory for Catechesis* reminds us, "…it is from the whole life of the Church that catechesis draws its legitimacy and energy" (#168).

The beliefs and practices for living the Catholic faith are embedded in the events of Church life. Event-centered faith formation prepares all ages and generations to understand the meaning of Church events and participate more consciously and actively in the life of the Church. In proposing the Christian community as the "source, *locus*, and means of catechesis" the *General Directory for Catechesis* affirms an events-centered approach to faith formation, making the content within the Church event and the community's participation in the event the primary means of faith formation (see GDC #158).

Far too many Catholics do not understand the central events of the Catholic tradition and Church life, are not prepared to participate in the life of the Church, and do not participate in the faith community. The power of the faith community and its events to form and transform people is dramatically reduced. An events-centered faith formation addresses these issues by reshaping the curriculum and the focus of learning programs around Church events, and by encouraging participation of all generations by making participation in parish life—the centerpiece of faith formation in Sunday Mass, the Church year feasts and seasons, sacramental celebrations and Church rituals, prayer traditions and devotions, the works of justice and acts of service.

We can discern five distinct types of events in the life of the parish community around which a lifelong curriculum can be fashioned. These events provide the clearest and most consistent structure for the lifelong faith formation of a parish community. They provide a regular ordering of Church life.

1. *Church year*: the Sunday Eucharist and the proclamation of the word of God through the year in the lectionary, and the celebration of the seasons, feasts, festivals, ethnic traditions, and saints' days of the liturgical year.

2. *Sacraments and life-cycle rituals*: the celebrations of the sacraments and Church rituals, such as funerals.

3. *Prayer traditions and spiritual practices*: the prayer of the community through prayer traditions such as the Stations of Cross, devotions such as Eucharistic adoration, and prayer traditions and practices of the Church year.

4. *Justice and service*: the ministries and projects of the local and national Church's work of justice and service to those in need, both locally and globally, the message of justice in the lectionary and Church year feasts and seasons, lives of justice and service in saints' feast days.

5. *Community life*: events in the life of the community such as gatherings, ethnic festivals, and parish anniversaries.

The content for lifelong faith formation—the beliefs and practices for living as a Catholic today—emerge from the events of the faith community. The beliefs and practices for living the Catholic faith are embedded in the events of Church life. The key catechetical task is to uncover the theological and doctrinal message within the event. The "content" emerges out of the event.

Consider the themes embedded in Lent: baptism, salvation, sin and repentance, conversion, cross, Jesus Christ, messiah and suffering servant, justice, moral life, paschal mystery, and the three lenten practices of fasting, praying, and almsgiving. A lifelong curriculum moves through these themes over multiple years, immersing people more deeply into the lenten experience. While every Church event is not as rich as Lent, the content that emerges from a six-year, event-centered curriculum provides the foundations of the Catholic faith.

A Lifelong Systematic Curriculum for the Whole Parish Community

Lifelong, events-centered faith formation views curriculum in a different way than the schooling, classroom paradigm. Curriculum in the schooling paradigm focuses exclusively on children and teenagers. It structures the content of the Catholic faith thematically in topics that are organized into sequential sessions and units by grade levels. The curriculum is produced in printed textbooks or other educational materials that parishes use to instruct children and teenagers. Publishers produce scope and sequence charts to present their systematic curriculum, a curriculum that is found in printed texts.

The word "curriculum" is derived from the Latin verb *currere*, which means to run. In literal terms, a curriculum is a course to be run. Curriculum is much broader than instruction and printed texts. As Maria Harris writes,

> we can conclude that fuller and more extensive curriculum is already present in the church's life: in teaching, worship, community, proclamation, and outreach. Printed resources that serve this wider curriculum are in the treasury of the church, especially the comprehensive curricular materials designed over the last century in the United States. These, however, are not the curriculum. The curriculum is both more basic and more profound. It is the entire course of the Church's life, found in the fundamental forms of that life. It is the priestly, prophetic, and political work of didache, leiturgia, koinonia, kerygma, and diakonia. Where education is the fashioning and refashioning of these forms in interplay, curriculum is the subject matter and processes that make them to be what they are. Where education is the living and the fashioning, curriculum is the life, the substance that is fashioned. (*Fashion Me a People*, p. 63-65)

The content for a curriculum can come from a source other than printed texts; it can come from the very life of the Church. In the words of Maria

Harris, curriculum is "the entire course of the Church's life." There are other ways to be systematic without adopting a schooling paradigm. For example, the Sundays, seasons, and feasts of the Church year systematically present the story of Jesus' life, deeds, teachings, death, and resurrection in word, symbol, ritual, prayer, music, and tradition. It is a cyclical curriculum. Each year we are invited to enter the story more deeply and appropriate its meaning into our lives in new ways.

The curriculum of lifelong faith formation is the Church itself. Out of the events of Church life, parishes fashion a foundational or core curriculum for the whole community. A lifelong curriculum systematically and comprehensively presents the gospel message and Catholic tradition using the events of Church life organized into six major curriculum themes: 1. Church year feasts and seasons, 2. the Creed, 3. sacraments, 4. morality, 5. justice, and 6. prayer. These curriculum themes incorporate the essential catechetical content set forth in the *Catechism of the Catholic Church*.

The *General Directory for Catechesis* (#115) affirms the significance of these six core themes of the Christian message:

- Church Year Feasts and Seasons:

  The history of salvation, recounting the "marvels of God" (*mirabilia Dei*), what He has done, continues to do and will do in the future for us, is organized in reference to Jesus Christ, the "center of salvation history" (DCG [1971], 41). (GDC #115) (See also GDC #85, 97–98, 101, 102, 105, 108.)

- Creed:

  The Apostles' Creed demonstrates how the Church has always desired to present the Christian mystery in a vital synthesis. This Creed is a synthesis of and a key to reading all of the Church's doctrine, which is hierarchically ordered around it.[97] (GDC #115) (See also GDC #85, 99–100, 108.)

  97. St. Cyril of Jerusalem affirms with regard to the Creed: "This synthesis of faith was not made to accord with human opinions but rather what was of the greatest importance was gathered from all the Scriptures, to present the one teaching of the faith in its entirety. And just as a mustard seed contains a great number of branches in a tiny grain, so too the summary of faith encompassed in a few words the whole knowledge of the true religion contained in the Old and New Testaments."

- Sacraments:

  The sacraments, which, like regenerating forces, spring from the paschal mystery of Jesus Christ, are also a whole. They form "an organic whole in which each particular sacrament has its own vital place" (CCC 1211). In this whole, the Holy Eucharist occupies a unique place to which all of the other sacraments are ordained. The Eucharist is to be presented as the "sacrament of sacraments." (*ibidem*). (GDC #115) (See also GDC #85, 108.)

- Morality:

The double commandment of love of God and neighbor is—in the moral message—a hierarchy of values which Jesus himself established. "On these two commandments depend all the Law and the Prophets" (Mt 22:40). The love of God and neighbor, which sum up the Decalogue, are lived in the spirit of the Beatitudes and constitute the magna carta of the Christian life proclaimed by Jesus in the Sermon on the Mount.[100] (GDC #115) (See also GDC #85, 97, 104, 108.)

100. St. Augustine presents the Sermon on the Mount as "the perfect charter of the Christian life and contains all the appropriate precepts necessary to guide it" (De Sermone Domini in Monte I, 1; Patrologiae Cursus completus, Series Latina 34, 1229-1231); cf. EN 8.

- Justice and Service:

Jesus, in announcing the Kingdom, proclaims the justice of God: he proclaims God's judgment and our responsibility....The call to conversion and belief in the Gospel of the Kingdom—a Kingdom of justice, love and peace, and in whose light we shall be judged—is fundamental for catechesis. (GDC #102) (See also GDC #86, 102–104, 108.)

- Prayer and Spirituality:

The Our Father gathers up the essence of the Gospel. It synthesizes and hierarchically structures the immense riches of prayer contained in Sacred Scripture and in all of the Church's life. (GDC #115) (See also GDC #85, 108.)

An events-centered approach should not be confused with a lectionary-based approach to faith formation. An events-centered approach utilizes the whole of Church life as its curriculum in order to teach the essential catechetical content set forth in the *Catechism of the Catholic Church*. Events-centered faith formation necessarily includes the lectionary as an integral element of the curriculum, but the scope of the curriculum is broader than the lectionary.

The events-centered lifelong curriculum provides for the authentic presentation of the Christian message as outlined in the *National Directory for Catechesis*.

The word of God contained in Sacred Scripture and Sacred Tradition is the single source of the fundamental criteria for the presentation of the Christian message. The presentation of the Christian message:

- Centers on Jesus Christ
- Introduces the Trinitarian dimension of the Gospel message
- Proclaims the Good News of salvation and liberation
- Comes from and leads to the Church
- Has a historical character
- Seeks inculturation and preserves the integrity and purity of the message
- Offers the comprehensive message of the Gospel and respects its inherent hierarchy of truths
- Communicates the profound dignity of the human person
- Fosters a common language of the faith. (NDC 25, p. 75)

These six curriculum themes are fashioned into a six-year curriculum plan, which provides the time to explore the foundations of Catholic faith with breadth and depth. The lifelong curriculum is a spiral curriculum with a six-year rotation of the major content areas. The events of Church life are so theologically rich that the "repetition" of the events provides people with an opportunity to develop a deeper understanding of the event and how to live its meaning in their lives.

The six-year curriculum is also developmentally appropriate. People learn with more depth at each stage of the life cycle as they move through the curriculum. Children who begin the six-year cycle in first grade will be adolescents (grades 7-12) when the next curriculum rotation begins, and young adults (ages 18-24) for the next spiral, and so forth. At each stage of life they will explore the same events and content in age-appropriate ways with increasing depth and application of learning.

Fashioning a Lifelong Curriculum

The faith formation curriculum in most parishes today is made up of age-specific programming for children, teens, and adults, and sacramental preparation for Christian Initiation (RCIA), baptism, confirmation, Eucharist, reconciliation, and marriage. Parishes have structured their faith formation curriculum to address specific learning needs of people at different stages of the life cycle or to prepare people for sacraments. By focusing on specific learning needs of groups, parishes have been able to specialize and target their learning programs.

Over the past three decades there has been dramatic development and improvement in age-group and sacramental catechesis. However, age-specific and sacramental catechesis is not designed to provide lifelong faith formation for the parish community. Every parish needs a lifelong core curriculum for the whole parish community that provides the heart of the parish's curriculum.

The central task for parish faith formation today is to develop a total curriculum that integrates the lifelong core curriculum for the whole parish community with age-specific curricula for children, adolescents, and adults to form one comprehensive, parish-wide curriculum. This will provide common learning experiences for all generations, and age-appropriate learning experiences that address the life cycle-specific learning needs of individuals. The diagram below seeks to visualize the interdependence of the core curriculum with age-specific and targeted curricula.

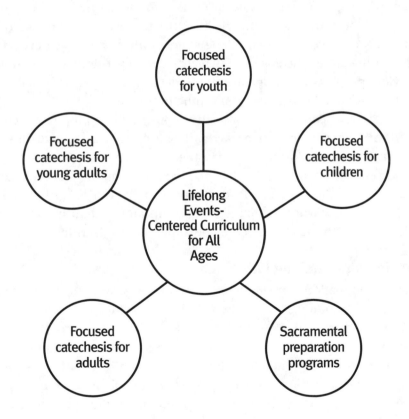

What would a six-year, events-centered, core curriculum for the whole parish community look like? Here is an example of a curriculum fashioned out of the events of Church life, organized around the six curriculum themes. It is one example of the variety of ways a parish can fashion a lifelong curriculum. As you read this example, make special note of how the curriculum is sequenced around the pattern that already exists in a local church. Events and doctrinal themes have been selected to provide the foundations of the Catholic faith for the whole parish community.

A Year of Church Year Feasts and Seasons

December	Advent Season (Preparing for the Messiah)
December	Christmas Season (Birth of the Messiah)
January	Feast of the Baptism of the Lord (Mission of Jesus)
February	Lenten Season (Three Practices: Praying, Fasting, Almsgiving)
March	Good Friday (Death of the Messiah)
April	Easter Season (Resurrection of the Messiah)
May	Feast of Pentecost (Mission of the Church)
June	Feast of Corpus Christi (Body of Christ)
August	Feast of the Assumption (Mary, Mother of Jesus)
September	Sundays (Identity of Christ)
October	Sundays (Living as a Disciple)
November	Feast of All Saints (Communion of Saints)

A Year of Creed

December	Incarnation (Christmas)
January	Jesus, Son of God (Baptism of the Lord)
February	Forgiveness of Sins (Lent)
March	Paschal Mystery: Death and Resurrection (Triduum)
April	Resurrection: New Life in Christ (Easter Season)
May	Holy Spirit (Pentecost)
June	Trinity and God the Father (Trinity Sunday)
June	Church (Feast of Saints Peter and Paul)
July-September	Jesus, Son of God (Transfiguration, 21st Sunday-Year A, 24th Sunday-Year B, 30th Sunday-Year A, 31st Sunday-Year B)
November	Resurrection of the Dead (All Saints and All Souls)
November	Kingdom of God (Christ the King)

A Year of Sacraments

December	Reconciliation (Parish Celebration)
January	Eucharist (Theme: Four Movements of the Mass)
February	Marriage (World Marriage Day and Anniversary Celebrations)
March	Baptism (Lent and Easter Vigil)
April	Liturgy of Eucharist (Holy Thursday and First Eucharist Celebrations)
May	Holy Orders (World Vocation Day)
June	Confirmation (Parish Celebration of Confirmation)
August-September	Liturgy of the Word (Sundays of Ordinary Time)
October	Anointing of the Sick (Parish Celebration)
November	Rite of Funerals (Feast of All Souls)

A Year of Morality

December	Fourth, Sixth, and Ninth Commandment: Faithfulness (Holy Family Sunday)
January	Moral Values: Sermon on the Mount or Plain (4th–9th Sundays-Year A or 6th–8th Sundays-Year C)
February	Conscience and Moral Decision-Making (Lent)
March	Care, Compassion, and Forgiveness (Sacrament of Reconciliation in Lent)
April	Care for God's Creation (Earth Day)
May-June	Moral Values: Sermon on the Mount or Plain (4th–9th Sundays-Year A or 6th–8th Sundays-Year C)
September	Seventh and Tenth Commandment: Justice (Rich Man and Lazarus: 26th Sunday-Year C or Christ the King-Year A in November)
October	Fifth Commandment: Respect for Human Dignity (Respect Life Sunday)
October	First Commandment: Love of God (30th Sunday-Year A)
November	Eighth Commandment: Honesty and Integrity (Feast of All Saints)

A Year of Justice and Service

December	Christmas and January 1: World Day of Peace (Peace)
January	Poverty Awareness Month (Rights and Responsibilities)
February	Lent (Solidarity with the Poor)
March	Good Friday (Sacrificial Love)
April	Earth Day (Care for God's Creation)
May	Feast of Pentecost (Solidarity with People around the World)
June-August	Summer Service Projects and Immersion Trips (Option for the Poor and Vulnerable)
September	Labor Day (Dignity of Work and Rights of Workers)
October	Respect Life Month (Dignity of the Human Person)
November	All Saints Day (Lives of Justice: The Saints)

A Year of Prayer

December	Prayer in the Advent and Christmas Seasons
January	Catholic Prayers and Devotions
February	Prayer in the Lenten Season
March	Prayer in Holy Week
April	Praying as a Community: Eucharist (Easter Season)
May	Our Father (Easter Season)
June-September	Praying with Scripture and the Lectionary (Ordinary Time)
October	Praying the Rosary
November	Praying with the Saints (Feast of All Saints)

The lifelong, events-centered curriculum provides a foundational, systematic faith formation which presents the gospel message and Catholic tradition to the whole parish community and engages the community in experiencing events within the life of the parish. The fundamental unity of the parish is strengthened by establishing a common focus for faith formation that engages all members of the community in learning through parish programs, at home, and through Sunday Mass and the events of parish life.

Chart 1 at the end of this chapter provides the scope of foundational events that are included in a lifelong curriculum. Three of the curriculum themes—Church year, sacraments, and prayer—begin with events then identify a doctrinal theme. Three of the curriculum areas—creed, morality, and justice—begin with the particular teaching and then identify potential events that embody the teaching.

In addition to the foundational events of Church life, parishes also incorporate events and themes that reflect the character, culture, history, and people of their community. This inculturates the curriculum in the local parish community. Here is an example of one year in the life of an African-American parish community in Buffalo, New York. They fashioned one year of their curriculum around events that shape and form their identity as African-American Catholics.

September	Council of Elders/Grandparents (Role of Elders in the African-American Culture)
October	Columbus Day (Middle Passage)
November	Feast Day of St. Martin de Porres
December	Kwanza (Holy Family)
January	Christian Unity Sunday (Christianity and Diversity)
February	Remembrance of Josephine Bakhita (Slavery)
March	Palm Sunday: Community Procession of Palms (Wearing Your Faith for All to See)
April	Earth Day (Celebration of God's Creation)
May	Corpus Christi Sunday (We Are One Body)
September	Feast Day of St. Peter Claver (Caring and Compassion)

The Lifelong Curriculum in Practice

As part of the total parish faith formation curriculum, parishes utilize the lifelong curriculum in two fundamental ways. In the first approach, parishes utilize the events-centered curriculum as the primary faith formation for the whole parish community, supported by limited age-group catechesis. In the second approach, parishes blend the core curriculum with school-year age-group catechesis, usually organized weekly.

Primary Curriculum Approach

Parishes that implement the primary curriculum approach fashion a curriculum plan that incorporates eight or more events per year. In the primary approach the curriculum must provide all the foundations or essentials of the Catholic faith for all ages and generations. Age-group faith formation is refocused to address faith themes and learning needs not addressed in the lifelong curriculum.

Adopting a primary approach does not affect the broader ministry with children, teens, and adults. It moves much of the catechesis for age groups into the lifelong curriculum for the whole parish community, but other ministry programming remains unaffected. For example, a parish youth ministry can focus its energy on the other important components of youth ministry, knowing that much of the catechesis for teens is being addressed in the lifelong curriculum. Programs such as monthly youth gatherings, retreats, social events, and summer service continue. Adult Bible study groups continue to meet and explore Scripture together. Children continue to perform in the Christmas pageant and participate in vacation Bible school. Age-group programming complements the primary, lifelong curriculum and enhances it by providing additional programs and ministry opportunities for specific age groups.

Sacramental preparation programs, such as first Eucharist and first reconciliation, continue as a focused catechesis for those preparing to celebrate the sacrament. Confirmation preparation and RCIA preparation programs are enhanced by incorporating the lifelong curriculum into these preparation programs. For example, each month catechumens can participate in the intergenerational learning program with other adults, while learning in their catechumenal group the other weeks of the month. The monthly intergenerational learning program and participation in Church events become part of the catechumenal preparation. Catechumens have the opportunity to learn with the whole parish community and to see firsthand that learning is for a lifetime. A lifelong curriculum can help address the challenge of engaging the newly baptized in mystagogy since it provides continuous learning for adults.

Parishes that adopt a primary approach offer monthly, events-centered, intergenerational programs as their principal learning model. They usually eliminate weekly age-group sessions during the school year, replacing them with targeted programming that addresses age-group learning needs not incorporated in the lifelong curriculum. Parishes have developed a variety of innovative approaches to provide age-group learning that does not involve weekly classes, including:

- *Monthly sessions.* Monthly sessions can be utilized to extend and deepen the learning from the monthly, events-centered, intergenerational learning program. For example, a parish can offer three "going deeper" sessions each month—one for children or families, one for teens, and one for adults. These sessions provide an opportunity to explore more deeply the content introduced in the monthly intergenerational program. Monthly sessions can also be utilized to provide thematic catechesis utilizing a textbook series or program resource that presents age-appropriate learning. For example, a parish can use a textbook series for children and middle school teens with seven units or major faith themes each year, and conduct seven monthly sessions, one for each unit or theme. This same thematic approach can be used for high school teens and adults.

- *Extended programs.* One-day or weekend programs provide another setting focused learning on faith themes particular to an age group. For example, several one-day programs or twice-a-year overnight or weekend programs can provide middle school or high school youth with an in-depth exploration of a particular faith theme, such as Scripture, the life of Jesus, the sacraments, or moral values and decision-making. A retreat day, two or three times a year, for families with children can provide much of the content currently being taught in weekly classes. The retreat days can be combined with the use of a textbook for home learning sessions to extend the learning and provide continuity throughout the year.

- *Summer weeklong programs.* Parishes can utilize the very successful vacation Bible school format to provide age-group learning for children and younger teens. Sessions can be structured around the content of a textbook series or other program resource. In addition to the sessions, the program would include prayer, community building, creative arts activities, recreation, and a family component.

- *Home learning.* Several publishers provide home learning sessions online to accompany their textbook series. Home learning moves the focus of children's learning from the parish to the family. A parish can conduct a one-day workshop for parents to teach them the skills for home learning and how to use the textbook with their children. The family's participation in monthly intergenerational learning provides a support system for home learning and reinforces what is being taught at home. Parishes can gather parents and/or the whole family with seasonal learning sessions to complement home learning.

- *Small group sessions.* Parishes can provide age-specific faith formation for young adults and adults through a small group learning
  model. These small group sessions can grow out of the monthly
  intergenerational learning programs, where young adults and
  adults are already learning in small groups. A small group format
  provides a way to extend the learning from the intergenerational
  session or to address faith themes that are especially relevant to
  young adults and adults.

Blended Curriculum Approach

Parishes that implement the blended approach integrate an events-
centered curriculum for all generations with school-year, age-group catechesis for children and youth. Parishes create one curriculum that blends
age-group catechesis with monthly or seasonal intergenerational, events-
centered learning programs, adjusting the number of sessions of age-
group catechesis to incorporate the intergenerational programs into the
yearly calendar. It also requires adjusting the content addressed in age-
specific catechesis to eliminate any overlap between events-centered catechesis and age-group catechesis. In the blended approach there is one
curriculum consisting of events-centered and age-group catechesis. Some
of the content is addressed through intergenerational, events-centered
learning for the whole community, while other content is addressed
through age-group catechesis.

There are three basic approaches for integrating an events-centered curriculum for the whole community with school-year, age group catechesis:
1. extending a theme in age-group catechesis to the whole parish community, 2. expanding a theme in age-group catechesis to the whole parish
community, and 3. replacing a theme in age-group catechesis with events-
centered learning for everyone (see Chart 2 for examples of each approach).

- *Extending.* Start with the units and learning sessions in children's
  catechesis and expand the topic or theme to the whole parish community. The events-centered curriculum can introduce or follow a
  theme in the children's catechetical program. For example, a unit
  on Jesus Christ in the children's program can be extended to the
  whole parish by focusing on a Church year feast or season or on a
  Sunday lectionary reading that correlates well with the content in
  the children's program. Conduct an intergenerational learning program that involves all ages and generations in learning about Jesus
  and prepares all to participate in the selected event.

- *Expanding.* Expand on topics in children's catechesis through events-centered learning for the whole parish community. For example, many of the children's catechetical programs provide supplemental sessions on Church year feasts and seasons, incorporating one or more years of events-centered, intergenerational learning on the Church year to expand on the learning in the children's program. The same approach can apply to prayer and justice, which are included in a children's program, but could be addressed more thoroughly through events-centered, intergenerational learning.

- *Replacing.* Replace a theme in the children's program with events-centered learning on the same theme for the whole parish community. For example, the unit on sacraments in the children's program can be replaced by multiple intergenerational sessions on sacraments throughout the year for all members of the parish community. Or an intergenerational session on one sacrament can replace a session in the children's catechetical program.

Parishes that adopt the blended approach often build up the number of events in their lifelong curriculum over several years, eventually incorporating as many as eight to ten events each year in their curriculum plan.

Conclusion

There are literally hundreds of ways to fashion a lifelong, events-centered curriculum and integrate it with age-group learning. Each parish needs to fashion its total parish curriculum around the life, character, culture, history, and people of its own community. This inculturates the curriculum in the local parish community, where people experience Church and the events of Church life. The foundational events of Church life (see Chart 1) provide a framework from which parish communities can fashion a curriculum that best reflects who they are and who they want to become.

For Fashioning a Lifelong Curriculum

Roberto, John. **Generations of Faith Resource Manual**. New London, CT: Twenty-Third Publications, 2005 (see Chapters 3 and 4).

Works Cited

Congregation for the Clergy. **General Directory for Catechesis**. Washington, DC: USCCB Publishing, 1997.

Harris, Maria. **Fashion Me a People: Curriculum in the Church**. Louisville, KY: Westminister/John Knox Press, 1989.

United States Conference of Catholic Bishops. **National Directory for Catechesis**. Washington, DC: USCCBB Publishing, 2005.

For Further Reading

Foster, Charles. **Educating Congregations**. Nashville: Abingdon, 1994.

Harris, Maria. **Fashion Me a People: Curriculum in the Church**. Louisville, KY: Westminster/John Knox Press, 1989.

Events and Catechetical Themes for a Lifelong Systematic Curriculum

Chart 1 provides the scope of foundational events that are included in a lifelong curriculum. Three of the curriculum themes—Church year, sacraments, and prayer—begin with events and then identify a doctrinal theme. Three of the curriculum areas—creed, morality, and justice—begin with the particular teaching and then identify potential events that embody the teaching.

Church Year

The history of salvation, recounting the "marvels of God" (*mirabilia Dei*), what He has done, continues to do and will do in the future for us, is organized in reference to Jesus Christ, the "center of salvation history" (DCG [1971] 41). (GDC #115) (See also GDC #85, 97–98, 101, 102, 105, 108.)

Who has encountered Christ desires to know him as much as possible, as well as to know the plan of the Father which he revealed. Knowledge of the faith (*fides quae*) is required by adherence to the faith (*fides qua*) (cf. DCG [1971] 36a). Even in the human order the love which one person has for another causes that person to wish to know the other all the more. Catechesis, must, therefore, lead to the "gradual grasping of the whole truth about the divine plan" (cf. DCG [1971] 24), by introducing the disciples of Jesus to a knowledge of Tradition and of Scripture, which is *"the sublime science of Christ"* (*Dei Verbum* [DV] 25a). (GDC #85)

Events	Themes and CCC References
Advent Season Christmas Christmas Season	Advent in Word, Ritual, and Symbols: Lectionary and Sacramentary Incarnation: CCC 422-443, 456-469, 479, 478, 483, 522-534 Jesus Christ, Messiah: CCC 436-40, 528-29, 702, 711-16 Salvation History: CCC 51-73, 430-40 Mary, Mother of Jesus: CCC 963-975
Feast of the Holy Family	CCC 525-534 Family: CCC 2201-2233
Feast of the Epiphany	CCC 528
Feast of the Baptism of the Lord	CCC 535-537 Kingdom of God: 541-550 Son of God: CCC 422-483 Sacrament of Baptism: CCC 1213-1274
Sundays of Ordinary Time (Jan-Feb)	Call of the disciples: CCC 425, 535-537, 541-542, 551-553, 787-788, 1223-1225
Lenten Season	Practices of Lent: CCC 1434, 2464, 2443-2449, 2558-2758 Conversion: CCC 541-546, 1427-1433, 1886-89, 1896, 2581-2584, 2608-2609 Sacrament of Reconciliation: CCC 1422-1484 Sin and Repentance: CCC 386-87, 1846-76 Lent in Word, Ritual, and Symbols: Lectionary and Sacramentary
Triduum	CCC 571-658 Triduum in Word, Ritual, and Symbols: Lectionary and Sacramentary
Holy Thursday	Eucharist: CCC 1322-1414 Holy Thursday in Word, Ritual, and Symbols: Lectionary and Sacramentary
Good Friday Stations of the Cross	Paschal Mystery: CCC 571-573, 599-618, 638-58 Passion and Death of Jesus: CCC 571-630 Salvation: CCC 218, 430-31, 456-57, 541-50, 620-22, 1019, 1811, 1816 Good Friday in Word, Ritual, and Symbols: Lectionary and Sacramentary

Events	Themes and CCC References
Easter Vigil	Salvation: CCC 218, 430-31, 456-57, 541-50, 599-605, 620-22, 1019, 1811, 1816 Paschal Mystery: CCC 571-573, 599-618, 638-58 Baptism: CCC 535-37, 1213-45, 1262-74 Resurrection: CCC 638-658 Easter Vigil in Word, Ritual, and Symbols: Lectionary and Sacramentary
Easter Sunday Easter Season	Resurrection: 638-658 Easter Season in Word, Ritual, and Symbols: Lectionary and Sacramentary
Feast of Pentecost	Holy Spirit: CCC 687-747 Pentecost in Word, Ritual, and Symbols: Lectionary and Sacramentary
Trinity Sunday	Trinity CCC 232-267 Trinity Sunday in Word, Ritual, and Symbols: Lectionary and Sacramentary
Sundays of Ordinary Time	Identity of Christ: CCC 422-483, 512-682, 702,711-16
Sundays of Ordinary Time	Living as a Disciple: CCC 541-550, 763-65, 768, 2816-282
Feast of the Annunciation Feast of the Assumption Feast of the Immaculate Conception Feast of the Our Lady of Guadalupe	Mary, Mother of Jesus: CCC 484-511, 721-726, 963-975
Feast of All Saints	Communion of Saints: CCC 946-962
Feast of All Souls	Resurrection of the Body and Life Everlasting: CCC 1020-102
Feast of Christ the King	CCC 783-786

Sacraments and Church Rituals

The sacraments, which, like regenerating forces, spring from the paschal mystery of Jesus Christ, are also a whole. They form "an organic whole in which each particular sacrament has its own vital place" (CCC 1211). In this whole, the Holy Eucharist occupies a unique place to which all of the other sacraments are ordained. The Eucharist is to be presented as the "sacrament of sacraments" (CCC 1211). (GDC #115) (See also GDC #85, 108.)

Christ is always present in his Church, especially in "liturgical cele-brations" (*Sacrosanctum Concilium* [SC] 7). Communion with Jesus Christ leads to the celebration of the salvific presence in the sacra-ments, especially in the Eucharist. The Church ardently desires that all the Christian faithful be brought to that full, conscious and active participation which is required by the very nature of the litur-gy (cf. SC 14) and the dignity of the baptismal priesthood. For this reason, catechesis, along with promoting a knowledge of the mean-ing of the liturgy and the sacraments, must also educate the disci-ples of Jesus Christ "for prayer, for thanksgiving, for repentance, for praying with confidence, for community spirit, for understanding correctly the meaning of the creeds...," (DCG [1971] 25b) as all of this is necessary for a true liturgical life. (GDC #85)

Sacraments and Suggested Events	Themes and CCC References
Baptism Easter Vigil Celebration of Baptism Feast of the Baptism of the Lord	Theology of Baptism: CCC 1213-1274 Paschal mystery: CCC 571-73, 599-618, 638-58 Mission of Jesus: CCC 430, 436, 438, 534, 536, 606, 608 Conversion: CCC 541-46, 1427-33, 1886-89, 1896, 2581-84, 2608-09 Sin and repentance: CCC 386-87, 1427-60, 1846-76 Witness: 897-913 Baptism in Word, Ritual, Symbols: Rite of Baptism and Rite of Christian Initiation of Adults
Confirmation Celebration of Confirmation Easter Vigil Pentecost	Theology of Confirmation: CCC 1285-1321 Holy Spirit: CCC 687-747 Gifts and charisms: CCC 878-95, 799-801, 1830-32 Witness: 897-913 Confirmation in Word, Ritual, and Symbols: Rite of Confirmation

Eucharist Sunday Eucharist Holy Thursday Easter Season Emmaus Story: 3rd Sunday of Easter-A Feast of Corpus Christi Celebration of First Eucharist	Theology of Eucharist: CCC 1322-1405 The Third Commandment: CCC 2168-2195 Bread and wine: CCC 1329, 1333-36, 1375-76, 1406, 1413 Four Movements of the Mass: Sacramentary and Lectionary Liturgy of the Word: Lectionary Liturgy of the Eucharist and Real Presence: Sacramentary
Reconciliation Parish Celebration of Reconciliation Celebration of First Reconciliation	Theology of Reconciliation: CCC 1422-1484 Sin and Repentance: CCC 386-87, 1846-76 Conversion: CCC 541-546, 1427-1433, 1886-89, 1896, 2581-2584, 2608-2609 Moral life: #1699-1729, #1776-89, #1830-45, #1965-1964 Reconciliation in Word, Symbol, Ritual: Rite of Reconciliation
Anointing of the Sick Parish Celebration of Anointing of the Sick	Theology of Anointing of the Sick: CCC 1499-1525 Anointing of the Sick in Word, Symbol, Ritual: Rite of Anointing of the Sick
Marriage Celebration of Matrimony World Marriage Day Holy Family Sunday Parish Remembrance of Anniversaries	Theology of Marriage: CCC 1601-1658 Love of Husband and Wife: CCC 2360-2379 Family: CCC 2201-2233 Marriage in Word, Symbol, Ritual: Rite of Marriage
Holy Orders Celebration of Ordinations to Priesthood and Deaconate Anniversary of Ordinations World Day of Prayer for Vocations	Theology of Ordination: CCC 1536-1589 Holy Orders in Word, Ritual, Symbols: Rite of Ordination
Rite of Funerals Celebration of the Rite of Funerals All Souls Day Sundays with Lectionary readings on dying and rising such as Raising of Lazarus (5th Sunday of Lent-A)	Christian Funerals: #1680-1690 Communion of Saints: #946-48, #956-57, #2683 Resurrection of the body: #988-1014 Life everlasting: #1020-1050 Rite of Funerals in Word, Ritual, Symbols: Rite of Funerals

Creed

The Apostles' Creed demonstrates how the Church has always desired to present the Christian mystery in a vital synthesis. This Creed is a synthesis of and a key to reading all of the Church's doctrine, which is hierarchically ordered around it.[97] (GDC #115) (See also GDC #85, 99–100, 108.)

Who has encountered Christ desires to know him as much as possible, as well as to know the plan of the Father which he revealed. Knowledge of the faith (*fides quae*) is required by adherence to the faith (*fides qua*) (cf. DCG [1971] 36a). Even in the human order the love which one person has for another causes that person to wish to know the other all the more. Catechesis, must, therefore, lead to the "gradual grasping of the whole truth about the divine plan (cf. DCG [1971] 24)," by introducing the disciples of Jesus to a knowledge of Tradition and of Scripture, which is "the sublime science of Christ" (DV 25a). By deepening the knowledge of the faith, catechesis nourishes not only the life of faith but equips it to explain itself to the world. The meaning of the creed, which is a compendium of Scripture and of the faith of the Church, is the realization of this task. (GDC #85)

97. St. Cyril of Jerusalem affirms with regard to the Creed: "This synthesis of faith was not made to accord with human opinions but rather what was of the greatest importance was gathered from all the Scriptures, to present the one teaching of the faith in its entirety. And just as a mustard seed contains a great number of branches in a tiny grain, so too the summary of faith encompassed in a few words the whole knowledge of the true religion contained in the Old and New Testaments."

Creedal Beliefs & Suggested Events	Themes & CCC References
THE TRINITY Trinity Sunday	CCC 232-267
GOD THE FATHER AND CREATOR Easter Vigil and Easter Season Trinity Sunday Sacrament of Baptism	I believe in God the Father: CCC 199-324
JESUS CHRIST, SON OF GOD Advent Season Christmas Season Feast of the Baptism of the Lord Feast of the Transfiguration: 21st Sunday–Year A 21st Sunday–Year A and 24th Sunday–Year B	I believe in Jesus Christ, the only Son of God: CCC 422-534

JESUS CHRIST: DEATH AND RESURRECTION	Jesus Christ suffered under Pontius Pilate, was crucified, died, and was buried: CCC 571-682
Triduum Liturgies: Holy Thursday, Good Friday, and Easter Vigil Easter Season Ascension Feast of the Triumph of the Cross Christ the King—Years B and C	I believe in the resurrection of the body: CCC 988-1019
HOLY SPIRIT Easter Season Feast of Pentecost Sacrament of Baptism Sacrament of Confirmation	I believe in the Holy Spirit: CCC 687-747
THE CHURCH Easter Season Feast of Pentecost Feast of Sts. Peter and Paul	I believe in the holy Catholic Church: CCC 758-870
COMMUNION OF SAINTS AND LIFE Everlasting Feast of All Saints Feast of All Souls	The communion of saints: CCC 946-962 I believe in life everlasting: CCC 1020-1029

Morality

The double commandment of love of God and neighbor is—in the moral message—a hierarchy of values which Jesus himself established. "On these two commandments depend all the Law and the Prophets" (Mt 22:40). The love of God and neighbor, which sum up the Decalogue, are lived in the spirit of the Beatitudes and constitute the *magna carta* of the Christian life proclaimed by Jesus in the Sermon on the Mount.100 (GDC #115) (See also GDC #85, 97, 104, 108.)

Conversion to Jesus Christ implies walking in his footsteps. Catechesis, must, therefore transmit to the disciples the attitudes of the Master himself. The disciples thus undertake a journey of interior transformation, in which, by participating in the paschal mystery of the Lord, "they pass from the old man to the new man who has been made perfect in Christ" (AG 13). The Sermon on the Mount, in which Jesus takes up the Decalogue, and impresses upon it the spirit of the beatitudes,[8] is an indispensable point of reference for the moral formation which is most necessary today....This moral testimony, which is prepared for by catechesis, must always demonstrate the social consequences of the demands of the Gospel (cf. CT 29f). (GDC #85)

100. St. Augustine presents the Sermon on the Mount as "the perfect charter of the Christian life and contains all the appropriate precepts necessary to guide it" (*De Sermone Domini in Monte* I, 1; *Patrologiae Cursus completus, Series Latina* 34, 1229-1231); cf. EN 8.

31. Cf. LG 62; CCC 1965-1986. The CCC 1697 specifies in particular the characteristics which catechesis must assume in moral formation.

Moral Principles & Suggested Events	Themes & CCC References
LOVE OF GOD AND NEIGHBOR Great Commandment: 30th Sunday–Year A Sermon on the Mount (4th–9th Sundays– Year A Sermon on the Plain (6th–8th Sundays–Year C Good Samaritan: 15th Sunday-Year C	The Law of the Gospel: CCC 1965-1974 Ten Commandments: CCC 2052-2055 The First Commandment: CCC 2083-2109
RESPECT FOR HUMAN DIGNITY Respect Life Sunday Feast Days of Saints Justice Events and Service Projects	The Fifth Commandment: CCC 2258-2330
JUSTICE Sermon on the Plain: 6th–8th Sundays–Year C Rich Man and Lazarus: 26th Sunday–Year C Feast of Christ the King–Year A Justice Events and Service Projects Feast Days of Justice Saints	The Seventh Commandment: CCC 2401-2463 The Tenth Commandment: CCC 2534-2557 Virtue of Justice: CCC 1807 Common Good: CCC 1905-1912 Social Justice: CCC 1928-1948
FAITHFULNESS Sacrament of Marriage World Marriage Day Feast of the Holy Family Sunday Lectionary Readings	The Sixth Commandment: CCC 2331-2400 The Ninth Commandment: CCC 2514-2553
HONESTY AND INTEGRITY Feast Days of Saints Sunday Lectionary Readings	The Eighth Commandment: CCC 2464-2513
CARE, COMPASSION, AND FORGIVENESS Sacrament of Reconciliation Sacrament of Anointing of the Sick Sunday Lectionary Readings: Jesus' Ministry of Healing and Forgiveness Justice Events and Service Projects	Jesus' ministry: CCC 543-550 Forgive us our trespasses: CCC 2838-2845 Sacrament of Reconciliation: CCC 1422-1484 Sacrament of the Anointing of the Sick: CCC 1499-1525

Justice

Jesus, in announcing the Kingdom, proclaims the justice of God: he proclaims God's judgment and our responsibility....The call to conversion and belief in the Gospel of the Kingdom—a Kingdom of justice, love and peace, and in whose light we shall be judged—is fundamental for catechesis. (GDC #102) (See also GDC #86, 102–104, 108.)

Catechesis is also open to the missionary dimension (cf. CT 24b and DCG [1971] 28). This seeks to equip the disciples of Jesus to be present as Christians in society through their professional, cultural and social lives....The evangelical attitudes which Jesus taught his disciples when he sent them on mission are precisely those which catechesis must nourish: to seek out the lost sheep, proclaim and heal at the same time, to be poor, without money or knapsack; to know how to accept rejection and persecution; to place one's trust in the Father and in the support of the Holy Spirit; to expect no other reward than the joy of working for the Kingdom (cf. Mt 10:5–42 and Lk 10:1–20). (GDC #86a)

Justice Teachings and Suggested Events	CCC References
DIGNITY OF HUMAN LIFE Respect Life Sunday Feast Days of Saints Local, National, and International Justice Events and Service Projects	CCC 1929-1938, 2259-2283 The Gospel of Life (Pope John Paul II)
RIGHTS AND RESPONSIBILITIES Church Year: Advent Season, Lenten Season, and Christ the King–Year A Thanksgiving Poverty Awareness Month (Jan) Migrant and Refugee Week (Jan) Feast Days of Saints Local, National, and International Justice Events and Service Projects	CCC 1905-1917, 2459 Economic Justice for All (USCCB)
SOLIDARITY Church Year: Lenten Season and Feast of Pentecost Mission Sunday Feast Days of Saints Local, National, and International Justice Events and Service Projects	CCC 1939-1942, 2438 Called to Global Solidarity (USCCB)

OPTION FOR THE POOR Church Year: Advent Season, Lenten Season, Our Lady of Guadalupe, Las Posadas, Christ the King–Year A, and 26th Sunday–Year C Thanksgiving Poverty Awareness Month Migrant and Refugee Week Feast Days of Saints Local, National, and International Justice Events and Service Projects	CCC 2443-2449 A Place at the Table: A Catholic Recommitment to Overcome Poverty and to Respect the Dignity of All God's Children (USCCB) Economic Justice for All (Tenth Anniversary Edition) (USCCB)
CARE FOR GOD'S CREATION Church Year: Easter Season Earth Day and World Environment Day Feast of St. Francis of Assisi Local, National, and International Environmental Projects	CCC 339, 295, 299, 2415-2418 Renewing the Earth (USCCB)
PEACE Church Year: Advent Season and Christmas World Day of Peace Martin Luther King, Jr. Remembrance Feast Days of Saints Local, National, and International Peace Projects	CCC 2302-2317 Confronting a Culture of Violence (USCCB) The Challenge of Peace (USCCB) The Harvest of Justice is Sown in Peace (USCCB)
CALL TO FAMILY, COMMUNITY, AND PARTICIPATION Holy Family Sunday Local, state, and national elections Justice, advocacy, and service Projects	Family: CCC 2201-2233 Citizens: CCC 2238-2243 Economic Justice for All (USCCB)
DIGNITY OF WORK AND RIGHTS OF WORKERS Labor Day Feast of St. Joseph the Worker	Economic Justice for All (USCCB)

Prayer and Spirituality

The Our Father gathers up the essence of the Gospel. It synthesizes and hierarchically structures the immense riches of prayer contained in Sacred Scripture and in all of the Church's life. (GDC #115) (See also GDC #85, 108.)

Communion with Jesus Christ leads the disciples to assume the attitude of prayer and contemplation which the Master himself had. To learn to pray with Jesus is to pray with the same sentiments with which he turned to the Father: adoration, praise, thanksgiving, filial confidence, supplication and awe for his glory. All of these sentiments are reflected in the *Our Father*, the prayer which Jesus taught his disciples and which is the model of all Christian prayer. The *"handing on of the Our Father"* (RCIA 25 and 188-191) is a summary of the entire Gospel (cf. CCC 2761) and is therefore a true act of catechesis. When catechesis is permeated by a climate of prayer, the assimilation of the entire Christian life reaches its summit.... (GDC #85)

Prayer Themes and Suggested Events	Themes & CCC References
CALL TO PRAYER: FORMS AND EXPRESSIONS OF PRAYER Sunday Mass Prayer Traditions and Practices World Day of Prayer Feast Days of Saints: Praying in the Traditions of the Saints	CCC 2556-2565, 2623-2649, 2650-2682, 2697-2724
THE LORD'S PRAYER Sunday Mass 17th Sunday–Year C	CCC 2759-2865
PRAYING THROUGH THE YEAR: ADVENT AND CHRISTMAS SEASONS Advent Season Christmas Season Sacrament of Reconciliation Praying with the Daily Lectionary Lectio Divina and Liturgy of the Hours	CCC 2558-2565, 2623-2649, 2650-2682, 2697-2724
PRAYING THROUGH THE YEAR: LENT AND EASTER SEASONS Lenten Season Sacrament of Reconciliation Stations of the Cross Triduum Liturgies Easter Season Praying with the Daily Lectionary Lectio Divina and Liturgy of the Hours	CCC 2558-2565, 2623-2649, 2650-2682, 2697-2724

THE ROSARY Feast Days of Mary Praying the Rosary through Year: Joyful (Christmas Season), Sorrowful (Holy Week), Glorious (Easter Season), Luminous (Ordinary Time)	CCC 2558-2565, 2623-2649, 2650-2682, 2697-2724
CATHOLIC PRAYERS AND DEVOTIONS Lectio Divina and Liturgy of the Hours Eucharistic Adoration Parish prayer services Sign of the Cross Stations of the Cross Prayer traditions of the saints	CCC 2558-2565, 2623-2649, 2650-2682, 2697-2724

Chart 2

Examples of Blended Curriculum

Here are several sample curriculum plans that integrate children's catechesis with event-centered, intergenerational catechesis. For purposes of the following examples, the children's program uses the four pillars of the *Catechism of the Catholic Church* as the four units covered each year.

Example 1: Extending a Theme

The following chart demonstrates one way to blend Church year feasts and seasons with the existing curriculum and calendar of the children's program. An intergenerational learning program for Church year feasts or seasons can extend or expand the children's theme. For example, the Advent season and intergenerational learning program can extend the focus on Jesus begun in Unit 1 with topics such as preparing for the Messiah and John the Baptist, or images of the Messiah from the Hebrew Scriptures and the gospels. Lent can extend Unit 3 on morality by focusing on conscience, sin, and reconciliation. You can also expand to new themes in Church year events not covered in the children's programs.

September-October	Weekly Classes: Unit 1. Creed (6 sessions)
Late October	Feast of All Saints Intergenerational Program: Communion of Saints
November	Weekly Classes: Unit 2. Sacraments-Part 1 (3 sessions)
Late November	Advent Intergenerational Program: Preparing for the Messiah
December	Advent-Christmas Seasons (no classes)
January	Weekly Classes: Unit 2. Sacraments-Part 2 (3 sessions)
February	Weekly Classes: Unit 3. Morality-Part 1 (3 sessions)
Late February	Lenten Intergenerational Program: Three Practices
March	Weekly Classes: Unit 3. Morality-Part 2 (3 sessions)
Late March	Triduum Intergenerational Program: Paschal Mystery
Early April	Holy Week (no classes)
April-May	Weekly Classes: Unit 4. Prayer (6 sessions)
Late May	Pentecost Intergenerational Program: Holy Spirit

Example 2: Expanding a Theme

The following chart provides one way to develop events-centered, inter-generational catechesis that expands the children's program with a more thorough approach. This example focuses on justice and service, utilizing events throughout the year. Each event would be greatly enriched by adding local justice and service projects that provide ways for people of all ages to be involved in the work of justice.

September	Respect Life Sunday Intergenerational Program: Dignity of Human Life
October	Weekly Classes: Unit 3. Morality (6 sessions) (connected to Respect Life Sunday and theme)
November	Weekly Classes: Unit 1. Creed-Part 1 (3 sessions)
Late November	Thanksgiving Intergenerational Program: Option for the Poor and Vulnerable
December	Weekly Classes: Unit 1. Creed-Part 2 (3 sessions)
January	Poverty Awareness Month Intergenerational Program: Rights and Responsibilities
January-February	Weekly Classes: Unit 2. Sacraments (6 sessions)
Late February	Lenten Intergenerational Program: Solidarity and Service
March-April	Weekly Classes: Unit 4. Prayer (6 sessions)
Late April	Earth Day Intergenerational Program: Care for God's Creation

Example 3: Replacing a Children's Theme

The following two charts provide an example of how to replace a theme or unit in the children's program with an event-centered, intergenerational catechetical program. The first example focuses on sacraments, and the second on creed. This template could be used to replace any age-group faith theme with event-centered, intergenerational catechesis.

Example 1. Sacraments

September-October	Weekly Classes: Unit 1. Creed (6 sessions)
Early November	Anointing of the Sick Intergenerational Program (Parish Celebration in November)
Late November	Reconciliation Advent Intergenerational Program (Parish Celebration in December)
December	Advent-Christmas Seasons (no classes)

January	Holy Orders Intergenerational Program (Vocations Week)
January-February	Weekly Classes: Unit 3. Morality (6 sessions)
Late February	Baptism Intergenerational Program (Lenten Season)
March	Weekly Classes: Unit 4. Prayer-Part 1 (3 sessions)
Late March	Eucharist Intergenerational Program (Holy Thursday)
Early April	Holy Week (no classes)
April-May	Weekly Classes: Unit 4. Prayer-Part 2 (3 sessions)
Late May	Confirmation Intergenerational Program (Parish Celebration of Confirmation)

Example 2. Creed

September-October	Weekly Classes: Unit 2. Sacraments (6 sessions)
November	Feast of All Saints and All Souls Intergenerational Program: Communion of Saints and Life Everlasting
December	Christmas Intergenerational Program: Incarnation and Jesus Christ, Son of God
January-March	Weekly Classes: Unit 3. Morality (6 sessions) Weekly Classes: Unit 4. Prayer-Part 1 (3 sessions)
March	Triduum Intergenerational Program: Jesus Christ: Death and Resurrection
April	Weekly Classes: Unit 4. Prayer-Part 2 (3 sessions)
Early May	Pentecost Intergenerational Program: Holy Spirit
Late May	Trinity Sunday Intergenerational Program: Trinity and God the Father
June	Church Intergenerational Program: Feast of Saints Peter and Paul

Chapter Four

Practices of Lifelong Faith Formation

Intergenerational Learning
for the Whole Parish Community

An Events-Centered Learning Process

The *General Directory for Catechesis* envisions the baptismal catechumenate as a model of catechizing activity for all faith formation. The learning process in the baptismal catechumenate is intimately connected to the life of the Church. We can discern three movements in the process of learning:

- preparation for discipleship and full, conscious, and active participation in Church life (catechumenate);
- experience of Church life—the encounter with Jesus Christ, the Scriptures and the tradition—through Sunday liturgy, the sacraments, Church year feasts and seasons, justice and service, prayer and devotions, and eventually through the celebration of the sacraments of initiation;
- reflection on the significance and meaning of learning and application to living as a disciple at home and in the world (mystagogy).

Events-centered faith formation utilizes the same learning process for each event in a lifelong curriculum. All learning programs are directly connected to the life of the Church. What people learn in an intergenerational program is experienced at the Church event and lived out at home and in the world.

The events-centered learning process includes the following three movements:

1. *Prepare* people of all ages, through learning programs, for participation in the event of Church life. The content of the learning program comes out of the event itself. Preparation empowers people to participate meaningfully in the event; it tunes them in to the dynamic of the event. It provides the learning activities and resources that help people to learn what they need to know and be able to do in order to participate fully in the event. Preparation programs and activities are designed to help people of all ages and generations develop:

   - *know-what*, a fuller understanding of the event and its doctrinal focus;
   - *know-why*, a deeper understanding of the meaning and significance of the event for their lives as Catholics;
   - *know-how*, the ability to participate competently in the event and to live its meaning in their lives as Catholics.

2. *Engage* people in the Church event. Participation in the life of the Church is an "experience." It is the encounter with Jesus Christ, the Good News, the tradition of the Church, and the people of God. Events are at the heart of the learning process. People learn by actively participating in the event. Learning is fundamentally experiential and social. Etienne Wenger observes, "there is no distinction between learning and social participation, and that is what makes learning possible, enduring, and meaningful. Learning is most effective when it is integrated in a form of social participation." Craig Dykstra observes,

   > The process of coming to faith and growing in the life of faith is fundamentally a process of participation. We come to recognize and live in the Spirit as we participate more and more broadly and deeply in communities that know God's love, acknowledge it, express it, and live their lives in the light of it. (*Growing in the Life of Faith*, p. 40)

   Participation in the event is so central to the learning process that we can conclude that the failure to learn is the normal result of exclusion from participation. Lives are transformed when people encounter Jesus Christ and his community through participation in the life of the Church. Events-centered learning makes this central to the learning process.

3. Guide people in *reflecting* on the significance and meaning of their participation and learning, and in applying and living their faith at home and in the world. Reflection helps people to:
    - *share* their experience of the event;
    - *assess* the significance or meaning they draw from their engagement in the event and connect it to the Scriptures and Catholic tradition;
    - *apply* the meaning to their daily life in the form of new beliefs and/or practices for living.

The events-centered learning process can be diagrammed as a cyclic process:

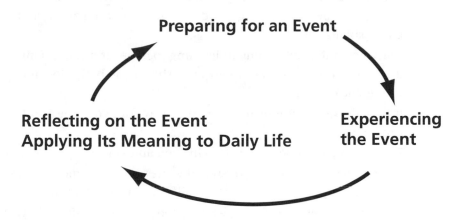

Preparing for an Event

**Reflecting on the Event
Applying Its Meaning to Daily Life**

**Experiencing
the Event**

Events-Centered Intergenerational Learning

The new paradigm of lifelong faith formation for the whole parish community needs to utilize a process that engages all generations in learning together. The adoption of intergenerational learning provides a model that gathers the whole parish to learn, build community, share faith, pray, celebrate, and practice their faith. The *General Directory for Catechesis* reminds us, "it should not be overlooked that the recipient of catechesis is the whole Christian community and every person in it" (GDC #168). Intergenerational learning prepares the whole community for meaningful participation in the life of the Church as well as living their Catholic faith at home and in the world.

Features of Intergenerational Learning

Intergenerational learning provides a new model of learning that produces important benefits for parish communities, families, and individuals. Here are several of the distinctive features of intergenerational learning:

1. It is inclusive of all ages and generations, single or married, with or without children.

2. It builds community and meaningful relationships across all generations in a parish.

3. It provides a setting for each generation to share and learn from other generations (their faith, stories, wisdom, experience, and knowledge). Parents and grandparents pass on the traditions of family and faith to younger generations, while younger generations share their faith, energy, and new insights with parents and grandparents.

4. It involves the whole family in learning together and equips families with knowledge, skills, and faith-sharing activities for nurturing faith at home.

5. It provides an environment where new ways of living one's faith can be practiced.

6. It provides adult role models for children and youth.

7. It promotes understanding of shared values and a common faith, as well as respect for individuals in all stages and ages of life.

8. It helps to overcome the age-segregated nature of our society, including parish programs.

9. It enhances people's identification with their parish and integration within the parish community.

10. It incorporates a variety of ways to learn: prayer, community building, interactive and experiential presentations and activities, group discussion, and sharing.

In the Spring of 2005, the Center for Ministry Development conducted a research study, using focus groups and in-depth interviews, in almost 100 parishes in eight dioceses that have been participating in the Generations of Faith project. Each parish in the study is conducting events-centered intergenerational learning programs monthly or seasonally. After careful analysis of the research, the following nine findings emerged from all diocesan groups as significant indicators of the impact and effectiveness of intergenerational learning.

1. There is involvement of all ages and generations—parents and children, teens, young adults, adults, older adults, and whole families—in faith formation through intergenerational learning.
2. Intergenerational relationships are created as people of all ages learn from each other and grow in faith together.
3. Intergenerational learning strengthened the parish community through relationship-building and participation in Church life. People take time to talk and share with each other.
4. Participation in intergenerational learning has led to greater involvement in parish life, including Sunday liturgy, parish events (justice projects, sacramental celebrations), and parish ministries.
5. Intergenerational learning addresses a hunger that adults have to learn more about their faith and fill in the gaps in their formation. More adults are participating in faith formation.
6. Families enjoy opportunities to pray, learn, and be together. Families are growing in the ways they share faith.
7. Intergenerational learning creates an environment in which participants feel safe to learn, ask questions, and grow in faith on a deeper level.
8. Participants are engaged in a variety of learning activities that are experiential, multi-sensory, and interactive. Faith sharing and personal experience are an important element of learning.
9. Intergenerational learning is exciting; the enthusiasm, joy, and energy are attractive and contagious.

Principles of Intergenerational Learning

Intergenerational learning incorporates a variety of methods and approaches that actively engage people in the learning process and respond to their different learning styles. There are seven essential principles that guide the design and facilitation of an intergenerational program.

Principle 1. Intergenerational learning programs balance affective, behavioral, and cognitive learning. Each program promotes learning in three dimensions:

- *know-what:* understanding the meaning of the event and its Scriptural, doctrinal, and theological foundation;
- *know-why:* appreciating and valuing the meaning and significance of the event for their lives as Catholics;

- *know-how:* acquiring the ability to participate competently in the event and to live its meaning in their lives as Catholics.

Principle 2. Intergenerational learning programs create an environment of warmth, trust, acceptance, and care that promotes group participation, activities, and discussion. Group participation encourages active, rather than passive, learning. Group activity engages participants in the learning process and makes them working partners with the catechist or facilitator. Lecturing is held to a minimum as highly participatory methods such as role-playing, simulated exercises, and case discussions are featured.

Principle 3. Intergenerational learning programs incorporate real-life application of learning by engaging people in the life of the parish community (events-centered) and helping people apply their learning to daily living as Catholics (home application). During the sessions, participants experience new ways to practice their faith, which promote the transfer of learning from the session to their daily lives as individuals and families.

Principle 4. Intergenerational learning programs utilize participants' experience and prior knowledge. In turn, participants bring relevant religious knowledge and experiences to the session. Participants have an opportunity to build on their knowledge, as well as to learn from each other.

Principle 5. Intergenerational learning programs respect the variety of learning styles among the participants. An effective intergenerational session actively engages learners in the learning process through a variety of learning methods and activities that address four fundamental learning styles.
- Some people learn best through direct, hands-on, concrete experiences. Intergenerational sessions engage the participants in the learning process either by connecting their life experience with their current understanding of the faith, or by providing them with an experience. To respect this learning style, sessions utilize methods such as story, film, drama and role-playing, music, personal story and sharing, prayer and ritual experiences, games or simulations, and real world problems or issue solving.
- Some people learn best through reflective observation. Intergenerational sessions engage the participants in reflecting on their personal, family, and religious experiences: what they notice about the experiences, where they find similarities and differences in people's experiences, what patterns reside in the experiences. To respect this learning style, sessions utilize methods such as personal reflection tools, small group sharing, compare and contrast activ-

ities, prayer activities (meditation and contemplation), and Scripture reflection activities.

- Some people learn best through an exploration and analysis of knowledge, theories, and concepts. Intergenerational sessions engage learners in understanding the scriptural and theological foundations of the Church event or theme. To respect this learning style, sessions utilize methods such as presentations of the foundational knowledge or teachings of an event or theme through a PowerPoint presentation, lecture, video, panel presentation, or through reading and discussing Scripture or brief theological articles or syntheses.

- Some people learn best through active experimentation with the new knowledge and practices. Intergenerational sessions engage learners in discovering ways to live out and apply their learning, especially by practicing what they have learned in the session. For example, if the goal of the session is to celebrate a Church year season at home, the session includes opportunities for people to practice the prayers, rituals, and activities that they are being given to use. To respect this learning style, sessions utilize methods such as action plans, in-session practice activities and exercises, personal evaluation and assessment tools, and take-home activities.

  (For further information see: *Experiential Learning: Experience as the Source of Learning and Development* by David Kolb. Englewood Cliffs, NJ: Prentice Hall, 1984.)

Principle 6. Intergenerational learning programs incorporate the theory of multiple intelligences and utilize different ways of learning. There is not just one type of intelligence; each learner has a unique combination of strengths and weaknesses. An effective intergenerational session capitalizes on these diverse strengths to enhance learning with methods and activities that address the variety of intelligences within a group. To do this, intergenerational sessions incorporate activities that address seven major intelligences. Here are examples of tools and activities than can be used with the different intelligences:

- For the "word smart": reading, storytelling, creative writing activities, presentations by learners, debates, demonstrations, drama, and role-playing.

- For the "logic smart": analyzing information and issues, puzzles, drawing, demonstration, debates.

- For the "picture smart": artwork, photographs, cartoons, collage, sculpture, drawing, illustrated story, video presentation, creative media projects, creative art projects.

- For the "music smart": singing, choral reading, film, creative music projects, drama, role-playing, prayer and ritual, creative audio or video projects.
- For the "body smart": drama, role-playing, puppets and puppet shows, dancing, painting, building or creating, demonstration, collage, ritual.
- For the "people smart": group activities, group discussion, interactive games, demonstrations and presentations, drama, and role-playing.
- For the "self smart": meditation, contemplation, journaling, creative writing projects.

  (For further information see the work of Howard Gardner; also *7 Kinds of Smart: Identifying and Developing Your Many Intelligences*, revised edition. Thomas Armstrong. New York: Plume Books, 1999.)

Principle 7. Intergenerational learning programs provide resources and activities for participants to continue their learning at home. The Home Kit is the centerpiece of the resources for both the home and the learning program. If we want people to feel confident, comfortable, and capable of using the home activities, then we need to use and model the activities in the session. If we want people to celebrate the home rituals included in the kit, then they need to experience one of the rituals in the session. If we want people to have a discussion at home, they need to experience how to have a discussion at the session.

If we want people to pray at home, they need to experience a prayer from the Home Kit during the session. By modeling in the session what we want to happen at home, we build up the confidence of families and individuals so that they can share, celebrate, and live faith at home. It is important to distribute the Home Kit at the beginning of the session so that participants work with the materials in the kit during the session.

The Design of Intergenerational Learning

Robert White defines intergenerational religious education as "two or more different age groups of people in a religious community together learning/growing/living in faith through in-common experiences, parallel learning, contributive-occasions, and interactive sharing" (*Intergenerational Religious Education*, p. 18). Intergenerational learning is designed around a four-movement learning process:

1. an all-ages learning experience for the whole assembly;
2. age-appropriate, in-depth learning experiences for families with children, adolescents, young adults, and adults;
3. an all-ages contributive learning experience in which each generation teaches the other generations;
4. reflection on the learning experience and interactive group sharing.

In an intergenerational design every part of the session contributes to the focus and objectives of the program from the meal and opening prayer through the closing prayer.

The intergenerational program has a moderate level of content that is explored and experienced using different learning methods and activities (recycling learning concepts).

Intergenerational learning programs are designed so that all ages can participate together in a common learning session. Each intergenerational session:

- combines intergenerational learning experiences with age-appropriate learning experiences for families with children (grades 1-5), adolescents, and adults;
- utilizes large group experiences with small group learning and sharing;
- is conducted in a three-hour time frame, with a meal included.

An essential element of the intergenerational design is family-centered learning for parents and children in grades 1 through grades 5 or 6. In Part 3: In-Depth Learning Experiences, parents and their children form a learning group. This provides one of the few opportunities that most families will have to learn together, share faith, pray, celebrate rituals and traditions, and live their faith. The learning activities are designed for whole family participation and often involve a table group of families.

Parents are the primary facilitators in family groups, guiding the whole family through the session plan. By leading the activities, such as reading Scripture, discussing a handout, developing a creative project, and praying, parents are growing in their own faith and developing skills for sharing and practicing their faith at home.

An essential component of a family learning session is faith enrichment for the parents through materials specifically designed for them. In many ways parents learn more than their children because they have a role in teaching the session. It is much easier to transfer the learning process to the home when the family has had a shared experience of learning and the parents have developed the skills and abilities for sharing faith.

Learning Process
Registration and Hospitality
Upon arriving at the learning program, participants are welcomed by the hospitality team. They then sign-in, make or receive a name tag, pick up their Home Kit and handouts for the session, and receive their learning group or table group assignments for the program. Depending on the time of day, the program may begin or end with a meal.

Part 1. Gathering and Prayer
The facilitator welcomes everyone, provides an overview of the learning program, and gives an introduction to the event and theme that is the focus of the program. Sometimes the teaching team leads the group in a community-building activity. The prayer and music team lead the opening prayer service.

Part 2. All-Ages Learning Experience
Each session has a multi-generational experience. All-ages learning experiences equalize the ages, so that listening to music, singing, watching a dramatic presentation, making an art project, watching a video, hearing a story, participating in a ritual, or praying together are things that different-aged people do at the same time and place in a similar manner. Shared experiences are absolutely critical for intergenerational learning.

Part 3. In-Depth Learning Experiences
Through structured learning activities and discussion all generations explore the meaning of the Church event and develop the ability to participate meaningfully in the event. Intergenerational learning programs include three sets of learning experiences for families with children in grades 1-5, adolescents, and adults. In-depth learning experiences can be conducted in one of three formats:
1. *Whole Group Format:* learning in small groups or table groups with the whole group assembled in one room.
2. *Age Group Format:* learning in separate, parallel groups organized by ages.
3. *Learning Activity Center Format:* learning at self-directed or facilitated activity centers.

The Whole Group Format provides a series of facilitated learning activities for everyone using a small group or table group format. Groups can be organized in one of two ways: intergenerational (mixed ages in a group) or age groups (separate groups for families with children, teens, young adults, and adults). A facilitator or team guides the entire group through an integrated learning program, giving presentations, leading activities, and so on. All presentations and activity instructions are given to the whole group. The age-appropriate learning activities are conducted in table groups. Where needed, catechists and small group leaders facilitate the work of the table groups.

The Age Group Format provides simultaneous age-appropriate learning for groups. Though age groups are separated, each one focuses on the same topic, utilizing specific learning activities that are designed for their life-cycle stage: families with children, adolescents, young adults, and adults. Catechists or facilitators lead the age-group sessions.

Age groups are organized in a variety of ways. The number of groups will vary depending on the number of participants and the available space in the parish facility. For example, if there are a small number of teens in grades 6-12, parishes can group them together for large group presentations and activities, then divide them into groups of grades 6-8 and 9-12 for reflection and discussion. Here is a suggested breakdown of age groups:

- 3 years old and younger: child care;
- 4 and 5 years old (including kindergarten): pre-school program with one or more catechists in a separate meeting space;
- parents with children in grades 1–5;
- middle school adolescents in grades 6–8;
- high school adolescents in grades 9–12;
- young adults (singles, married couples) from 18–39 years old;
- adults 40 years old and older.

The Learning Activity Center Format provides structured learning activities at a variety of stations or centers in a common area. Learning activity centers are self-contained learning experiences, focusing on a very specific topic or theme. They include brief presentations by the facilitators, interactive and experiential activities, group discussion and sharing. Each center can utilize a different learning method, such as drama, role-playing, creative arts, prayer, ritual, film, games, demonstrations, exhibits, or music.

One of the best ways to envision a Learning Activity Center Format is to imagine visiting a children's museum or one of the Epcot pavilions at Walt Disney World in Orlando. You will find a variety of interactive, experiential exhibits, media presentations, and staff-facilitated learning activities.

Learning Activity Centers can be used with all age groups. They can be developed for an intergenerational audience or for particular age groups, such as families with children or adolescents or adults. Learning Activity Centers can also be utilized in the families with children learning program within the Age Group Format.

The choice of the most appropriate learning format is determined by the content of the learning program, as well as the size and number of parish meeting rooms. From a facility perspective, the Age Group Format requires a large meeting space for the entire group and smaller meeting rooms for age-group sessions, while the Whole Group Format and Learning Activity Center Format only require a large meeting space.

From a design perspective, the content of the session can determine which learning format would work best. Here are three examples.

- For a creed and Church year session on the Triduum (theme: paschal mystery), the learning design provides an introduction to the liturgies of Holy Thursday, Good Friday, and Easter Vigil using a guided tour and experience of each liturgy. The learning format that works best for this content is the Whole Group Format because it keeps the whole group together for a common learning experience. The content for the session is the same; the learning activities are age-specific.

- For a justice session on rights and responsibilities, the learning design uses an Age Group Format to provide age-appropriate sessions for families with children, teens, and adults. The content of the session, Catholic social teaching, needs to be taught differently to each age group, so there are three lesson plans in the In-Depth Learning Experience. The focus of the session is the same, but the content and learning activities are age-specific.

- For a sacraments session on Eucharist, the learning design uses a Learning Activity Center Format with age-specific and intergenerational learning stations. Six activity centers can be developed:
    1. Liturgy of the Word: A Tour of What We Believe (all ages),
    2. Exploring a Eucharistic Prayer (adolescents and adults),
    3. Meal Stories (all ages, especially families with children),
    4. Creation of a Eucharist Table Cloth (all ages),
    5. Illustration of Eucharistic Prayer II (all ages),
    6. Bread Broken and Shared Reflection (all ages).

    The Learning Activity Center Format works best when the session does not require sequential development of the content (e.g., the four movements of the Mass or a guided tour of the Triduum), and when there are a variety of activities that can be utilized to teach the content (e.g., the large number of activities and resources that can be used for sessions about Advent and Lent).

Part 4. Sharing Learning Experiences and Home Application

The whole group gathers again, and each generation briefly shares what they have learned and/or created in their in-depth experiences. Whole group sharing provides an opportunity for each generation to teach the others. Groups can share the project or activity they created, offer a verbal summary or symbol of learning, or give a dramatic presentation. Whole group sharing can also be conducted in small intergenerational groups, rather than using presentations to the entire group.

To conclude the program participants have the opportunity to reflect on what they have learned and begin to apply this learning to their daily lives. This part of the program sends people home ready to participate in the upcoming event, as well as utilize the home activities.

The facilitator then reviews the Home Kit activities, such as prayers, rituals, service projects, family enrichment activities, and learning activities. Individuals and families then have time to create an at-home action plan for using the Home Kit.

Part 5. Closing Prayer Service

The session ends with a prayer service built around the theme of the event.

AN EXAMPLE

What does it look like when you put all the pieces together? Take a moment to follow along as All Saints Parish prepares for Lent.

The All Saints faith formation team has designed a variety of ways to prepare all of the generations for their participation in the lenten season. Their goal is to prepare everyone in the parish community for Lent, focusing on the theme for the year: "The Three Practices of Lent: Fasting, Praying, and Almsgiving." Preparation programs guide people of all ages to understand the meaning of Lent and the three practices, to appreciate the significance of Lent and the three practices in our Catholic tradition, to participate actively in the lenten season, and to live out the three practices at home and in the world. When people are prepared, they feel confident, comfortable, and competent to participate in the lenten season at home and in the parish.

An intergenerational learning program is one of the variety of learning approaches All Saints Parish is using to prepare all ages and generations for the lenten season. The week before Ash Wednesday—on a Wednesday night, Friday night, and Saturday morning—all ages and generations, from families with children through older adults, arrive at the parish center for a light dinner or continental breakfast, followed by the featured activity: learning how to live the three practices of praying, fasting, and almsgiving. The program moves through several stages of activities:

- Everyone gathers together for a meal, a great time to build community.
- The program begins with prayer and song inspired by the lenten season and the three practices. Music from the lenten liturgies is used in the prayer service. The focus of the Scripture reading is praying, fasting, and almsgiving (Matthew 6:1–6, 16–18, the Ash Wednesday gospel reading).
- An all-ages opening experience introduces everyone to the focus of preparation—the three practices of Lent—through story, drama, and media.
- The in-depth learning component of the program helps everyone explore the meaning of the event through age-appropriate learning groups. Families with children explore the lenten practices through three activity centers, one for each of the lenten practices. Adolescents explore the lenten practices and create contemporary ways to live out the three practices. A guest speaker presents an overview of the lenten lectionary readings and a contemporary interpretation of the lenten practices for adults.
- The entire group re-gathers to share with one another what they have learned from the in-depth sessions. This can be done in small intergenerational groups or through presentations to the entire group.
- One of the leaders shows how to use the lenten Home Kit, which provides resources for families and individuals to experience Lent at home: a lenten calendar with daily activities and Scripture passages; a lenten journal for teens with daily readings, prayers, and activities; a daily lenten prayer guide for adults; placemats with weekly table prayers; suggested local service projects and information about Operation Rice Bowl; several learning activities with lenten themes; and a copy of the parish's lenten calendar.
- In both family groups and adult groups, everyone develops a Lenten Pledge to live the three practices at home and in the world. Individual participants and families are given a lenten scrapbook to document their Lenten Pledge and forty-day journey from Ash Wednesday to Easter Sunday. The scrapbook can be filled with

photos, artwork, prayers, reflections, etc., documenting the "in-home" experience of Lent (e.g., photos of their times of prayer or involvement in serving others, copies of prayers used, copies of completed reflections, and so on). Participants are asked to bring their scrapbook back in two months so they can share what they have done and learned through their lenten experience.

- The program closes in prayer and song, once again inspired by the music and lectionary readings of Lent.

Examples of Events-Centered Intergenerational Programs

Here are three examples of intergenerational learning programs. Each example demonstrates one of the three learning formats in Part 3. In-Depth Learning Experiences of the intergenerational design.

Example 1. A Triduum Intergenerational Program

Theme: Paschal Mystery

Whole Group Learning Format

Here is an example of a three-hour intergenerational program to prepare the community for participation in the Triduum, focused on the theme of paschal mystery. Depending on the size of the parish, this program would be offered multiple times on evenings or weekends, one or two weeks before the Triduum. In this example, people are organized into intergenerational table groups for the whole program.

Part 1. Gathering and Opening Prayer

Part 2. All-Ages Learning Experience: Triduum Quiz

Test everyone's knowledge of the Triduum through an activity that matches symbols, ritual actions, and events from the lectionary readings with the correct Triduum liturgy.

Part 3. In-Depth Learning Experience

A. GUIDED TOUR OF HOLY THURSDAY

- Present the gospel story of the Last Supper from Matthew, Mark, or Luke in word, drama, and/or visuals (artwork or the film *Jesus of Nazareth*).
- Guide people in reflecting on the story. Provide commentary on the reading.
- Celebrate a table ritual modeled on the Last Supper.

- Present the gospel story of the Last Supper from John in word, drama, and/or visuals.
- Guide people in reflecting on the story. Provide commentary on the reading.
- Celebrate a table ritual modeled on the washing of feet with people washing each other's hands.

B. Guided Tour of Good Friday

- Present excerpts from the Passion of Christ from Matthew, Mark, or Luke in word, drama, and/or visuals.
- Guide people in reflecting on the Passion; provide commentary.
- Explain intercessory prayer and together, pray intercessions modeled on the Good Friday liturgy.
- Explain the tradition of the veneration of the cross. If possible, process around the meeting room carrying a cross, while people pray and sing.
- Guide people in making their own cross that they can use at home.

C. Guided Tour of the Easter Vigil

- Provide a brief overview of the major elements of the Easter Vigil liturgy.
- Celebrate a Service of Light modeled on the Easter Vigil and using the prayers from the Easter Vigil liturgy. Lead the group through the ritual and explanation of the symbols on the Easter Candle. Light individual candles and sing an appropriate song.
- Present selected lectionary readings with accompanying prayers from the Easter Vigil liturgy, for example:

  Genesis 1:1—2:2

  Exodus 14:15—15:1 (consider showing the crossing of the Red Sea scene from the movie *The Prince of Egypt*)

  Romans 6:3–11

  Gospel reading from the current liturgical year in word, drama, a dramatic reading with visual presentation, or film, such as *Jesus of Nazareth*

- Introduce the sacrament of baptism as central to the Easter Vigil liturgy and show how your parish initiates new members into the Church community every Easter. Guide people through the initiation rite: pray a short version of the Litany of the Saints, bless the bottles of water at each table, explain the celebration of baptism and confirmation, renew the baptismal profession of faith, sprinkle the people with holy water, and sing an appropriate song.

Part 4. Sharing Learning Experiences and Home Application

Part 5. Closing Prayer

- For the complete intergenerational program see: "Jesus Christ, Death and Resurrection" in *Professing Our Faith*, as well as "Death of the Messiah" in *Following Jesus* (Orlando, FL: Harcourt Religion, 2006).

Example 2. An Easter Season Intergenerational Program

Theme: New Life in Christ: Resurrection

Age Group Format

Here is an example of a three-hour intergenerational program to prepare the community for participation in the Easter season, focused on the theme of new life in Christ. Depending on the size of the parish, this program would be offered multiple times on evenings or weekends, one or two weeks before Easter. The session could also be offered right after Easter during Easter Week, since the Easter season lasts fifty days. The gospel stories form the core content for the session and are experienced multiple times: in prayer, in reading and discussion, in activities, and in life application.

Part 1. Gathering and Opening Prayer

Part 2. All-Ages Learning Experience: Scenes from the Easter Season Prayer Experience

Lead a prayer service focusing on the impact of the resurrection on the disciples and their conversion and commitment to Jesus. The prayer service incorporates scenes from the Easter Season lectionary readings using a freeze-frame approach to dramatizing the scenes. Create the props for each scene and ask the actors to dress for their parts in the stories. For each gospel reading, present the freeze-action, read the gospel, and respond in prayer.

Scene 1. Empty Tomb: Matthew 28:1–10 (Easter Vigil, Year A)

Scene 2. Closed Doors: John 20:19–31 (2nd Sunday of Easter, Year A)

Scene 3. Eating: John 21:9–17, 19 (3rd Sunday of Easter, Year C)

Scene 4. Commissioning: Matthew 28:16–20 (Ascension, Year A)

Part 3. In-Depth Learning Experiences:
Exploring the Resurrection (Age-Appropriate Learning)

- *Families with Children Learning Plan*

    Part 1. Explore the stories of the resurrection. Families read and discuss each of the four Easter gospel stories from the prayer experience.

    Part 2. Create an Easter banner. Families create a banner with key Scripture verses from the Easter readings, Easter symbols, and ideas for living the Easter season.

    Part 3. Decorate a family Easter candle. Families learn about the significance of the paschal candle and its symbols. They create a candle for their table at home with symbols of the Easter season and write a short prayer to pray each day at the family meal or gathering time.

- *Adolescent Learning Plan*

    Part 1. Explore the stories of the resurrection. Adolescents explore the gospel readings of the Easter season and discuss theological reflections on the readings.

    Part 2. Creative activities. Adolescents are engaged in one or more creative activities to bring the meaning of resurrection alive for them through a magazine story, a television report, a presentation, an advertisement, a top-ten list of reasons we know Jesus rose from the dead, and/or a debate on the importance of the resurrection.

    Part 3. Reflection activity on the Emmaus story.

- *Adult Learning Plan*

    Part 1. Explore the meaning of the resurrection. Adults reflect on their own understanding of the resurrection, and explore and discuss Church teaching, and theological reflections on the significance of the resurrection for the Catholic faith.

    Part 2. Grow in our relationship with Jesus Christ. Adults explore the meaning of the Emmaus story and use the story to reflect on their own relationship with Jesus.

    Part 3. Live the resurrection. Adults develop ways they can live out the Easter season in their lives.

Part 4. Sharing Learning Experiences and Home Application

Part 5. Closing Prayer

- For the complete intergenerational program see: "New Life in Christ" in *Following Jesus* (Harcourt Religion, 2005).

Example 3. Jesus, Son of God Intergenerational Program

Potential events: Christmas, Baptism of the Lord, Feast of the Transfiguration, 21st Sunday in Year A and 24th Sunday in Year B

Learning Activity Center Format

Here is an example of a three-hour intergenerational program to prepare the community for participation in an event that communicates Jesus' identity as the Son of God, such as Christmas. Depending on the size of the parish, this program would be offered multiple times on evenings or weekends, one or two weeks before the event. In this example, there are eight intergenerational learning activity centers that provide learning experiences to help people discover the qualities of God by exploring a variety of gospel stories that present the words and actions of Jesus Christ, the Son of God. Participants would have time to experience up to four activity centers during the session.

Part 1. Gathering and Opening Prayer

Part 2. All-Ages Learning Experience: Who Do You Say That I Am?
- Introduce the focusing question with a brief presentation.
- Have a short activity in which people name who Jesus is for them.

Part 3. In-Depth Learning Experiences:
Experiencing the Son of God through Gospel Stories
1. The focus of the activity centers is to discover the qualities of God by exploring a variety of gospel stories that present the words and actions of Jesus Christ, the Son of God.
2. Each learning activity center provides an interactive and experiential way for people to explore one aspect of Jesus' divinity through gospel stories.
3. Activity centers will explore the birth of Jesus and stories from the gospels, such as Jesus teaching the parables, being baptized, healing people, forgiving people, raising people from the dead, and feeding people.
4. Activity centers will engage participants in presentations, discussions, and activities. Several centers include dramatic presentations, while others will engage people in creative arts or prayer or a ritual activity. One center includes a film presentation, and there is even one that includes eating. If the children get tired, there is a storytelling center just for them.

5. Each center is staffed by a team who will guide participants through the learning activities.

6. Each center is designed for all ages, and participants can select the centers that interest them the most. Families with children should stay together.

ACTIVITY CENTERS

1. Jesus is Born (Infancy Narratives)
2. Jesus is God's Beloved Son (Baptism of the Lord and Transfiguration)
3. Jesus Teaches Parables of the Kingdom of God
4. Jesus Heals People
5. Jesus Forgives Sin
6. Jesus Raises People from the Dead
7. Jesus Feeds People
8. Stories of Jesus (Storytelling Center)

Part 4. Sharing Learning Experiences and Home Application

Part 5. Closing Prayer

- For the complete intergenerational program see: "Jesus Christ, Son of God" in *Professing Our Faith* (Harcourt Religion, 2005).

Incorporating Reflection in Events-Centered Learning

The third step of the learning process involves faith formation at home (see Chapter 5) and reflection on the entire learning experience: the intergenerational program, participation in the event, and practicing faith at home. In this final step of the learning process, parishes provide resources to guide people in reflecting on the significance and meaning of their participation and learning, and in applying their faith at home and in the world. Reflection is designed to help people:

- share their experience of the event,
- assess the significance or meaning they draw from their engagement in the event and connect it to the Scriptures and Catholic tradition, and
- apply the meaning to their daily lives in the form of new beliefs and/or practices for living.

Reflection can be facilitated at a parish gathering. Time for reflecting on the past month's events-centered learning can be incorporated into the opening activities of each intergenerational program, or it can be added after the conclusion of an event when people are already gathered.

Resources for family and individual reflection are included with the Home Kit that accompanies each intergenerational program. The Home Kit includes activities or strategies that help individuals and households reflect on the significance or meaning they draw from their engagement in the event and connect it to the Scriptures and Catholic tradition. It provides households with practical strategies and resources to apply what they have learned to daily life.

Reflection can take many forms:

- Written reflection activities such as unfinished sentences, learning journals, and a set of questions structured around the content of the event;
- Application activities such as an action plan, practice plan, pledge, and a "to-do" list;
- Art and media activities such as picture/photo collage or a poster demonstrating family faith practice, "recipe for living" cards with practices that families actually did, and a scrapbook of family faith practiced for the year.

Reflection can include opportunities for individuals and families to report or "publish" their learning through an activity that asks them to bring something back to the parish. For example, if families and individuals created a Lenten Pledge (fasting, prayer, and almsgiving ideas) during the intergenerational preparation program, they can bring back completed pledge with photos or other "documentation" to the Holy Thursday or Good Friday liturgies, or to the next intergenerational program.

Below are several reflection ideas to accompany an intergenerational program on the three practices of Lent: praying, fasting, and almsgiving.

- *Lenten journal:* Adolescents through adults, as well as families, can use journals to record their experience of Lent: their thoughts, feelings, questions, hopes, dreams, faith practices, and so on. Journals or poster-journals record the actual lenten practices of individuals and families. Families can create a poster-journal so that all family members can record their actions, thoughts, feelings, and what they have learned.
- *Lenten photo collage:* Parishes can provide each household with a disposable camera in their lenten Home Kit. Individuals and families take photos of their "in-home" experience of Lent, especially the three practices of Lent (e.g., a photo of the family at prayer or

serving others). Households prepare a photo collage that presents their experience of Lent with descriptions or captions that explain their actions and commentary on their feelings and/or thoughts about living Lent. They bring these back to Sunday Mass on a designated weekend to create a gallery of photo collages.

- *"Recipe for living" cards:* Individuals and families record their practical strategies for living out Lent on 3x5 file cards. People return the cards to the parish on one particular Sunday. Parishes can then produce a lenten "cookbook" of recipes for living the Catholic faith.

- *Lenten scrapbook:* Individuals and families create a small scrapbook to document their forty-day journey from Ash Wednesday to Easter Sunday. The scrapbook can contain photos, artwork, prayers, and reflections documenting the in-home experience of Lent. Parishes incorporate storytelling in the next intergenerational program so that individuals and families can share their stories of Lent through their scrapbooks.

Alignment of Learning

One of the important features of events-centered faith formation is that the whole parish is focused on the event: everyone is preparing for the same event with the same doctrinal focus. This is the practice of alignment of learning, i.e., using all of the ministries and programs of the parish to prepare the community for the event. The goal of alignment is that learning will permeate every aspect of parish life and create parish-wide synergy.

There are four primary ways to prepare the whole parish community for an event:

- formal learning through intergenerational programs and age-specific programs;
- embedded learning through parish meetings and programs;
- individualized learning through bulletin inserts, print and media resources, and the parish Web site;
- home learning through home activities and resources, and the parish Web site.

Designing a parish-wide learning plan for an event begins with identifying the potential audiences and settings—in addition to formal learning—that can be used to prepare people for an event. These audiences and settings will be particular to each parish, but they might include the following:

- adults in small faith-sharing groups and Bible study groups

- young adults through the Internet or e-mail
- older adults through parish gatherings and meetings
- the homebound
- parish leadership councils and committees
- parish ministry teams
- parish organizations such as men's and women's groups
- the congregation.

Using many of the resources and activities already designed for the intergenerational learning program and Home Kit, parishes can develop strategies and resources for reaching the different audiences within the parish community. For example:

- Use the opening prayer service and Scripture reading(s) from the intergenerational program at every parish meeting held during the entire month prior to the event.
- Bring the Home Kit to every homebound parishioner after each intergenerational program.
- Select resources from the session and Home Kit that you can publish on the parish Web site so that they are available to the entire parish.
- Develop a resource or activity from the intergenerational session or Home Kit that you can e-mail to young adults, such as weekly Scripture reflections during Advent or Lent.
- Include a newsletter or magazine in the parish bulletin to prepare the community for the event.

Alignment brings a focus to the parish's faith formation efforts focused on a common event. It insures that the whole parish is learning about the same thing at the same time. If a parish is intentional about alignment, the long-term result will be a more unified parish community that is continually learning through their common life together.

Works Cited

Dykstra, Craig. **Growing in the Life of Faith: Education and Christian Practices**. Louisville, KY: Geneva Press, 1998.

White, James. **Intergenerational Religious Education**. Birmingham, AL: Religious Education Press, 1988.

Wenger, Etienne and Jean Lave. **Situated Learning**. Cambridge: Cambridge University Press, 1991.

For Designing and Facilitating Intergenerational Learning

Martineau, Mariette. **People of Faith Organizer's Manual**. Orlando, FL: Harcourt Religion, 2005.

Roberto, John. **Generations of Faith Resource Manual**. New London, CT: Twenty-Third Publications, 2005 (see Chapter 5).

For Further Reading

White, James. **Intergenerational Religious Education**. Birmingham, AL: Religious Education Press, 1988.

Appendix 1

Additional Ways to Incorporate Intergenerational Learning into Parish Life

There are many ways to incorporate intergenerational learning into a parish community. Here are several additional strategies parishes can employ.

1. *Add intergenerational learning to sacramental preparation for baptism, first reconciliation, first Eucharist, confirmation, marriage, and RCIA.* The celebration of a sacrament for individual parishioners is an opportunity to enrich the faith of the whole community. For example, each year your parish can offer intergenerational learning for the whole parish community around the celebration of first Eucharist, focusing on the four movements of the Mass one year, the Real Presence of Christ in the Eucharist during the second year, and so forth. During the catechumenal formation of adult members of the community, the parish can offer intergenerational learning on initiation themes, such as the sacrament of baptism and conversion. This provides a way to involve the whole community in the journey of the catechumens.

2. *Conduct intergenerational learning for the parish community before the celebration of a sacrament.* The celebration of the sacraments of Eucharist, anointing of the sick, and reconciliation offer opportunities for parish-learning. Conduct intergenerational programs to prepare the parish community for the celebration of the sacrament of reconciliation in Advent or Lent, or the celebration of anointing of the sick at the weekend Masses.

3. *Conduct intergenerational learning before major Church year feasts and seasons, as well as parish events.* The parish calendar is rich with possibilities for intergenerational learning for the whole parish community. Conduct intergenerational programs around each of the major Church year feasts and seasons, for example, All Saints Day and All Souls Day, Advent, Christmas, Lent, Triduum, Easter, Pentecost, Trinity Sunday, the Feast of the Body and Blood of Christ Sunday; and around significant parish events, such as the parish anniversary, feast days of saints, and

stewardship Sunday or a parish ministries fair. There are dozens of parish-wide events that are opportunities for the whole parish community to participate more intentionally and meaningfully in parish events.

4. *Add intergenerational learning to a vacation Bible school or summer catechetical program.* Many parishes sponsor summer programs for children. This is another opportunity to hold an intergenerational learning program for the whole parish community. Take a theme from the summer program and offer an intergenerational program on that same theme for both families of the children and the parish community. For example, if the focus of the program is being a friend of Jesus, the parish can sponsor an intergenerational program on becoming a disciple or living as a disciple.

5. *Conduct intergenerational learning around local, national, and international justice events and project.* Parish, community, national, and international justice events and projects provide opportunities to engage the parish community in the work of justice, as well as learn about the principles of justice found in Scripture and Catholic social teaching. Prepare the parish community for a parish justice and service project, such as feeding and clothing the poor in your community, with an intergenerational program on the preferential option for the poor. Prepare the parish for Christmas and World Day of Peace (January 1) with an intergenerational program on peace. Engage the parish community in national and international justice projects, such as adopting a community development project in a developing country through Catholic Relief Services, with an intergenerational program on solidarity.

6. *Sponsor an intergenerational parish mission or parish retreat.* A parish mission is a great opportunity to enrich the faith of the whole parish community. Organize a parish mission for all ages and generations by conducting intergenerational sessions, rather than sessions for individual groups. Develop a focus for the mission, such as following Jesus, growing in prayer, or what we believe as Catholics. Select individual topics for each session of the parish mission and provide participants with home materials.

Using the same idea, a parish can conduct a day-long or weekend parish intergenerational retreat focused on an event or feast important to your parish community. Build a one-day retreat (6 hours), by using two intergenerational programs, and a weekend retreat by using multiple sessions along with community building activities, structured reflection times, prayer services, and Sunday Eucharist.

Chapter Five

Practices of Lifelong Faith Formation

Family and Household Faith Formation

At the heart of all faith formation is the family. "A family is our first community and most basic way in which the Lord gathers us, forms us, and acts in the world. The early Church expressed this truth by calling the Christian family a domestic Church or Church of the home" (*Follow the Way of Love*, p. 8). While the forms and structures of family life have changed dramatically, the fundamental reality remains: the family is the primary community of faith. It is a community with a distinct mission, "As Christian families, you not only belong to the Church, but your daily life is a true expression of the Church" (*Follow the Way of Love*, p. 8).

The family shares in the one and same mission that Christ gives to the whole Church. This mission includes loving God and each other, fostering intimacy, professing faith in God, setting an example of Christian living, praying together, serving, sacrificing for one another, forgiving and seeking reconciliation, celebrating life's passages, celebrating the sacraments, acting justly, and affirming life (see Appendix 1).

The *General Directory for Catechesis* places the family at the center of faith formation, affirming that the family is the "Church of the home" or "domestic church" and a unique locus for catechesis.

...in every Christian family the different aspects and functions of the life of the entire Church may be reflected: mission; catechesis; witness; prayer, etc. Indeed in the same way as the Church, the family "is a place in which the Gospel is transmitted and from which it extends." (EN 71) The family as a *locus* of catechesis has a unique privilege: transmitting the Gospel by rooting it in the context of profound human values. (cf. GS 52; FC 37a)...It is, indeed, a Christian education more witnessed to than taught, more occasional than systematic, more ongoing and daily than structured into periods. (GDC #255).

This vision of the family is reinforced by the *National Directory for Catechesis*:

The Christian family is ordinarily the first experience of the Christian community and the primary environment for growth in faith. Because it is the "church of the home" (FC 38), the family provides a unique *locus* for catechesis. It is a place in which the word of God is received and from which it is extended. Within the Christian family, parents are the primary educators in the faith and "the first heralds of the faith with regard to their children" (LG 11). But all the members make up the family, and each can make a unique contribution to creating the basic environment in which a sense of God's loving presence is awakened and faith in Jesus Christ is confessed, encouraged, and lived." (NDC 29D, pp. 100-101)

At every stage of the life cycle, the family, in its different faces and structures, is at the very heart of the new paradigm. What the *General Directory for Catechesis* and *National Directory for Catechesis* say about families can be applied to all households of faith throughout the life cycle—the new couple, families with children and teens, families with young adults, single adults, families in later life—and to all configurations of family relationships such as two-parent, single-parent, and multi-generational families. No longer an add-on to the work of faith formation, the family is now central to all faith formation efforts. Home and parish are linked in a comprehensive model of lifelong faith formation.

Of particular concern today are the parents of children and teens, adults in their late-twenties through forties, who grew up in a far more secular world, where the influence of Catholicism was much less evident than that of their parents and grandparents. They did not experience the culture of Catholicism that characterized generations of Catholics born before the 1960s. Consequently, many do not bring the knowledge and experience of the Catholic faith to their parenting and family life today. They also find themselves trying to share faith and values in a culture that is often hostile to the Catholic way of life. Parishes need to see this as an opportunity for faith formation and move beyond the attitude of blaming parents for a "lack of faith" at home. The future is in the hands of families, and they are looking to the Church to provide the wisdom and guidance, resources and support to live as Catholics in today's world.

How do parish communities nurture the faith of families throughout life, empower and equip them to learn and share the Catholic faith, celebrate rituals and traditions, pray, and live their faith at home and in the world? How do parish communities assist parents to develop the confidence, competence, and comfort to share the Catholic faith with their children? In the lifelong paradigm, the parish takes the initiative in nurturing the faith of families and empowering them to live their faith at home and in the world. This happens in four ways:

1. *Intergenerational learning.* By participating in intergenerational learning, families have a shared experienced of learning together, sharing faith, praying together, and celebrating rituals and traditions. The program models the faith practices and traditions that the parish hopes families will adopt. Families also learn the knowledge and skills for sharing faith, celebrating traditions, and practicing the Catholic faith at home. One of the primary goals of events-centered intergenerational learning is to equip families and individuals to apply their faith to life. When families learn together in the parish, they are empowered to learn together at home.

2. *Household faith practice.* Through home activities developed specifically for the event, families and households are given the resources they need to practice their faith at home. At an intergenerational program or in another learning setting, families receive home activities that are designed to help them integrate the Catholic faith into the fabric of home life, share faith around Scripture and the Catholic tradition, pray together and celebrate rituals as part of everyday life, care for each other and those in their community, work for justice and serve those in need both locally and globally. The Home Kit is an essential component of each events-centered learning plan. Home Kits are designed with activities for the entire household, as well as for particular age groups (children, teens, adults).

3. *Participation in Church life.* By participating in the life of the parish, especially Sunday Mass and the other events that are the focus of the curriculum, the faith of families is strengthened and

deepened. They experience the faith of the Church. They are connected to the parish community where they receive support and encouragement for living their faith.

4. *Household faith reflection.* Through reflection activities, families and individuals are given the resources to reflect on the meaning of their participation in the event, to connect it to what they have learned at the intergenerational program, and to consider how they live the Catholic faith at home, both as a family and as individuals.

The six-year, events-centered curriculum presented in the parish provides a pattern for developing the faith of families at home. It gives the structure and experiences for creating a pattern of faith sharing and practice that becomes integral to home life and is woven into the fabric of daily life. The parish can help every family develop a family faith calendar which incorporates Church events and home events into a pattern of faith practice that guides the family through the year. By utilizing the four tools outlined above, parishes can make a significant difference in empowering and equipping families to become faith-filled communities.

As noted by Gene Roehlkepartain in *The Teaching Church*, research by the Search Institute has identified five key factors that nourish faith maturity in families:

1. family faith conversations: talking about faith at home;
2. family devotions and worship: prayer, rituals, celebrations, Scripture reading;
3. family service projects: family involvement in helping others;
4. family education: parent education, family-centered or intergenerational catechesis;
5. parental relationships and parental faith.

These five factors can be translated into a framework for promoting faith at home and designing home activities. Home activities for an event should include as many of the following five elements as possible:

- *Learning*: helping families and individuals to develop the know-what and know-why of Church events, to explore Scripture and the Catholic tradition, and to apply faith to daily life as a follower of Jesus Christ.

- *Celebrating rituals*: helping families and individuals to develop patterns of ritual celebrations (daily, weekly, seasonally, annually) and celebrate Church events in a family way at home through a variety of ritual experiences for Church year feasts and seasons, weekly Sunday worship, sacraments, calendar year events, and milestones (birthdays, anniversaries, graduations, retirements).

- *Praying*: helping families and individuals to develop their prayer life and live the Church event through a variety of prayer experiences, such as morning and evening prayer, daily prayers for the season, table prayers, and traditional Catholic prayers.

- *Enriching relationships*: helping families strengthen family life by developing skills for family living, deepening the marriage relationship, and participating in family activities that build family strengths and celebrate family life.

- *Serving and working for justice*: helping families and individuals connect their involvement in Church events with the call to act justly and serve those in need, relate Scripture and Catholic social teaching to community and global social issues, engage in service to others and actions for social justice, and develop lifestyles based on gospel values.

A Curriculum for the Home

The family faith calendar is the equivalent of the parish's lifelong faith formation curriculum. It provides the pathway for family life. Home and parish share a common mission and curriculum.

> Your domestic church is not complete by itself, of course. It should be united with and supported by parishes and other communities within the larger Church. Christ has called you and joined you to himself in and through the sacraments. Therefore, you share in one and the same mission that he gives to the whole Church." (*Follow the Way of Love*, p. 8)

Imagine the long-term impact on families if a parish took seriously the home curriculum. Imagine the long-term impact on a parish if families were actively growing in faith at home. The new paradigm of lifelong, events-centered faith formation provides the structure for forging a partnership between home and parish, and helping families develop a pattern of faith practice at home. Here are several examples of the parish-home curriculum connections, using the themes of a lifelong curriculum.

Church Year

The Church year provides the first pattern for structuring the family faith calendar as the family journeys from Advent through the feast of Christ the King. A parish can provide home activities that equip families to incorporate the Church feast or season into home life using the five elements of family faith sharing: learning, celebrating, praying, enriching relationships, and serving and working for justice. Participation in intergenerational learning and the parish's celebration of the Church year encourages and supports family faith practice. Think of the possibilities for developing a family faith calendar around the following Church year feasts and seasons:

- Advent
- Christmas season, including the Feast of the Holy Family and Feast of the Epiphany
- Valentine's Day
- Lent
- Holy Week
- Easter Season
- Feast of Pentecost
- Feast of All Saints
- Feast of All Souls
- Thanksgiving
- Saints' feast days throughout the year

Here are examples of activities for all ages that can be included in an Advent/Christmas Home Kit that can be distributed at an Advent intergenerational program, or given to households each year, whether or not there is an intergenerational learning program for Advent or Christmas.

- *Prayer*: morning and nighttime prayers for December; prayers for every day of Advent; table prayers for Advent and the Christmas season; weekly prayers that can be used with an Advent wreath.
- *Rituals*: a blessing before the Christmas meal and for lighting the Christ candle; a blessing for a Christmas crèche; a blessing for a Christmas tree; a blessing to use when opening gifts; a ritual for the feast of Our Lady of Guadalupe.
- *Learning*: background, instructions, and materials for creating a Jesse Tree and/or an Advent wreath; day-by-day Advent calendars for children, teens, and adults; Advent reflection books for the whole family, teens, and/or adults; a list of Advent-Christmas storybooks and DVDs/videos; a guide to reading and exploring the Advent and Christmas lectionary.

- *Service*: a guide to Advent-Christmas service projects (collections of toys, food, or clothing, "adopt-a-family" projects); alternative gift-giving suggestions; a list of organizations for charitable donations.
- *Family enrichment*: recipes for family baking activities; ideas for making gifts; meal-time activities for the Advent-Christmas season.

Sacraments and Rituals

Sacraments and rituals provide a second pattern for structuring the family faith calendar, including

1. the parish's celebration of the sacraments through the year,
2. the family celebration of a sacrament, such as first Eucharist, and
3. the family's celebration of rites of passage and annual milestones, such as birthdays and anniversaries.

Participation in intergenerational learning, weekly Mass, and the parish's celebration of the sacraments encourages and supports family faith practice.

Every sacrament and life cycle ritual is an opportunity to nurture the faith of all generations in a family: grandparents, parents, children, teens, and young adults. Think of the possibilities for developing a family faith calendar around the following sacramental and ritual celebrations:

- Sunday Mass and the lectionary readings;
- Parish celebrations of baptism and Christian initiation, confirmation, reconciliation, and anointing of the sick;
- At-home celebrations and traditions around the sacramental celebrations of family members at baptism, first Eucharist, first reconciliation, confirmation, marriage, and/or the Rite of Christian Initiation of Adults;
- Continuing family faith formation (mystagogy) after the celebration of a sacrament, such as the years between baptism and first Eucharist;
- Family remembrances of baptismal anniversaries, marriage anniversaries, deaths of family members, and other significant sacramental moments in the life of the family;
- Family rituals for birthdays, anniversaries, and other milestones
- Rites of passage such as graduations, retirements, leaving home, the beginning and end of the school year.

Here are several examples for Home Kit activities that can accompany a sacramental celebration or participation in an intergenerational sacrament program.

EUCHARIST INTERGENERATIONAL PROGRAM HOME KIT

Theme: The Four Movements of the Mass

- *Learning*: short articles for adults, parents, and teens on Eucharist, such as those found in Catholic Updates (St. Anthony Messenger Press); a guide for children about the Mass; Scripture readings and reflections on the Eucharist; explanations of the symbols and ritual moments in Eucharist.

- *Prayer*: prayers before and after meals; seasonal table prayers for use during the year.

- *Rituals*: table rituals that use eucharistic themes; family meal traditions.

- *Service*: service projects that focus on feeding a hungry world.

- *Family enrichment*: ways to celebrate a family meal, ideas for making meal time special; tips for baking bread (recipe or bread mix) as a family activity.

SUNDAY EUCHARIST HOME ACTIVITIES

The weekly celebration of the Eucharist is an opportunity to empower families to live their faith both at home and in the world. Parishes can give families and individuals an activity, prayer, or ritual that extends the theme of the Sunday readings into the home. These activities can include age-appropriate learning activities to explore the gospel reading, a prayer that captures the theme of the liturgy, a ritual to enact at home, a symbol from the liturgy, family discussion questions, and ideas for living the Scripture message. For example,

- On the Sunday when we hear about Jesus multiplying the loaves and fishes, parishes can give each family a small loaf of bread or roll with a simple blessing. At home families can pray the blessing and break the bread at their Sunday meal and remember how the community broke bread at the eucharistic table.

- On Holy Family Sunday, the parish can pray a special blessing for families at Mass and provide families with a family commitment ritual they can use at home during their Sunday meal, or at another designated family time.

- On the Sunday when we hear about the rich man and Lazarus, parishes can provide everyone with a reflection activity about the gospel, information sheet about those in need, and a list of service projects.

- On the Sunday when we hear about the prodigal son, parishes can provide a family reconciliation ritual, reconciliation prayers and Scripture readings, and ideas for making peace at home and in the world.

BAPTISM HOME KIT

The following activities can be included in a Home Kit to accompany an intergenerational learning session on baptism or to accompany the celebration of baptism.

- *Learning*: Scripture readings and reflections on baptism; a guide to exploring the symbols of baptism; a Catholic Update on baptism; a list of children's storybooks; Bible stories; DVD/video and music suggestions for learning more about baptism.

- *Family enrichment* (for families celebrating baptism): resources for parenting children—skills, tools, information; family life activities such as making meal time special or family projects with young children.

- *Rituals*: the symbols of baptism—a small cross, bottle of holy water, candle, bottle of oil; ideas for creating a home altar with baptism symbols and pictures; a ritual for celebrating the anniversary of a baptism; a first book of family rituals (for new families).

- *Prayer*: table prayers for the anniversary of a baptism; table prayers for the symbols of baptism (water, light, oil); meal prayers on the themes of baptism; a first book of Catholic prayers and devotions (for new families).

- *Service*: ideas and activities for living one's baptismal call such as suggestions for developing a stewardship lifestyle, a guide to getting involved in parish ministries, ideas for service in the community and world.

Justice and Service

The Church's work of justice and acts of service—both locally and globally—provide another way to structure the family faith calendar. This happens in several ways.

First, as one of the five elements of family faith formation (Church year events, sacraments, morality themes, and creedal beliefs), justice and service activities are an integral part of Home Kits.

Second, justice and service is one of the six major curriculum themes in an events-centered, lifelong curriculum so intergenerational programs on justice events and themes will have Home Kits that provide resources for further learning and action projects for individuals and families. For example, the season of Lent can focus on the option for the poor, one of the principles of Catholic social teaching. The lenten practice of almsgiving and the lectionary readings for Lent, such as Isaiah 58, provide a solid grounding in the lenten season. The focus of the intergenerational learning program would be on Catholic social teaching and how to live the option for the poor during Lent and throughout the year.

The intergenerational Home Kit for Lent on the theme of the option for the poor can include the following types of activities:

- *Learning*: print and Web resources for further learning on poverty; readings and reflections on the preferential option for the poor found in Scripture; a summary of Catholic social teaching on the option for the poor; stories of saints who served the poor; stories of Catholic organizations, like the Campaign for Human Development and Catholic Relief Services, who serve the poor; a family magazine on the option for the poor (see *People of Faith: Generations Learning Together*, volume 1, issue 4).

- *Service*: "Action Projects Booklet" with descriptions of local, national, and global projects that individuals, families, and the whole parish community use to get involved in serving the poor.

- *Family enrichment*: purchasing fair trade products that assist workers in developing countries; getting involved as a family in a service project; eating a simple meal each week and giving the money to an organization that serves the needs of the poor.

- *Prayer*: prayers for every day of Lent with a focus on justice and option for the poor; table prayers for Lent.

- *Rituals*: an Ash Wednesday home ritual; a booklet for celebrating the Stations of the Cross as a family.

Third, the Church year, saints' feast days, the justice calendar of the Catholic Church, and national and global justice events and remembrances provide a variety of ways to structure the family faith calendar with justice and service events and projects. Parishes can prepare a booklet or information sheet with background on the event, ideas for celebrating or remembering the event (prayers and/or rituals), and action projects that families can undertake. If the parish has a Web site, this can be used to deliver the information and activities to families.

Think of the possibilities for developing a family faith calendar around the following justice and service events:

December	Advent lectionary readings on justice themes
December 1	World AIDS Day
December 2	Anniversary of the Deaths of Four North American Martyrs in El Salvador: Maura Clarke, Ita Ford, Dorothy Kazel, and Jeanne Donovan
December 10	Human Rights Day
December 12	Feast of Our Lady of Guadalupe
December 17-24	Las Posadas (hospitality and homelessness)
January 1	World Day of Peace
January	Migrant and Refugee Week (U.S. Catholic Bishops)
January	Poverty Awareness Month (U.S. Catholic Bishops)
January	Martin Luther King, Jr., Anniversary
January	March for Life
February-March	Lenten lectionary readings on justice themes
February-March	Operation Rice Bowl (Catholic Relief Services)
March 24	Archbishop Oscar Romero
Summer	26th Sunday-Year C (The Rich Man and Lazarus: Luke 16:19–31).
September 10	Mother Teresa
September 27	St. Vincent de Paul
October	Respect Life Sunday (U.S. Catholic Bishops)
October	Thanksgiving (Canada)
October 4	St. Francis of Assisi
October 16	World Food Day
November	Campaign for Human Development Sunday (U.S. Catholic Bishops)
November 3	St. Martin de Porres
November 26	Dorothy Day
November	Feast of Christ the King, Year A (Matthew 25:31–46)
November	Thanksgiving (U.S.)

Prayer, Creed, and Morality

The prayer life and tradition of the Church provides a fourth pattern for structuring the family faith calendar. The goal is to integrate prayer into the daily and seasonal patterns of family living. As one of the five elements of family faith formation, prayer is woven into the Home Kits and resources in the other curriculum themes: Church year, sacraments, justice, morality, and creed. These Home Kits include daily and seasonal prayers, table prayers, and prayers for family milestones and rites of passage. Home Kits that accompany intergenerational sessions on prayer include further learning about prayer, and actual prayer resources such as Catholic prayers and devotions, prayer forms, expressions, practices, and traditions. The Home Kit helps the family learn more about prayer while exposing them to a variety of prayer practices, such as *lectio divina*.

Fashioning a curriculum for creed and morality utilizes Church year feasts and seasons, the lectionary, the lives of the saints, sacraments and rituals, and justice events. These two curriculum themes would be integrated into a family faith calendar through other events. Home Kits that accompany intergenerational sessions on the creed and morality would utilize the five elements of family faith formation: learning, rituals, prayer, family enrichment, and justice.

Conclusion

At the heart of all faith formation is the family, the primary community of faith. There may be no greater challenge facing the Church today than nurturing families in the Catholic faith and empowering them to practice their faith at home and in the world. Helping families become communities of learning and practice will take years. For decades, families with children and adolescents have expected the parish or Catholic school to take on the faith formation of their children.

In the new paradigm, the expectation is that parish and home are partners in faith formation. This is a far more demanding approach for both parishes and households. Parishes are expected to make household faith formation a priority. It is built into the very fabric of lifelong, events-centered faith formation.

Parish communities are called to nurture the faith of families throughout life, and empower and equip them to learn and share the Catholic faith, celebrate rituals and traditions, pray, and live their faith both at home and in the world. Parish communities are called to assist parents in nurturing their own faith life so they develop the confidence, competence, and comfort to share the Catholic faith with their children.

Households are challenged to make faith a priority in their lives, to become of community of faith learning and practice. They are called to find God and the sacred in their home life. They are challenged to embrace their mission as the Church of the home. They are called to re-build or begin the process of building a household of faith with a pattern of learning, celebrating rituals and traditions, praying together, enriching their family relationships, and serving those in need. And they are not doing this alone. By participating in intergenerational learning and the life of the parish, they will be connected to the community of faith where they can experience support and encouragement for living the Catholic way of life.

This approach to family faith formation is more prescriptive in presenting the ways families can engage in faith learning at home. It begins with the events of Church life and builds a connection to the home. This approach will require intentional effort and time on the part of parish leadership because many families do not have the motivation and intention to grow in faith as a family. Motivation and intention do not come automatically. What is needed is an evangelization process whereby families are helped to recognize God's gracious activity in their lives and invited to respond to it. Helping families become intentional about their faith growth must be a priority in the parish, particularly for those engaged in intergenerational faith formation.[1]

These changes will take time. The loss of strong households of faith has taken decades, and will take years to rebuild them. But there is no more important task in faith formation today.

End Notes

1. A helpful resource on family faith formation is *Families and Faith: A Vision and Practice for Parish Ministry*, edited by Leif Kehrwald (Twenty-Third Publications, 2006), particularly Chapters Four and Five.

Works Cited

Roehlkepartain, Gene. **The Teaching Church**. Nashville: Abingdon Press, 1993.

United States Conference of Catholic Bishops. **Follow the Way of Love**. Washington, DC: USCC Publishing, 1994.

For Designing Home Activities

Martineau, Mariette. **People of Faith Organizer's Manual**. Orlando, FL: Harcourt Religion, 2005.

Roberto, John. **Generations of Faith Resource Manual**. New London, CT: Twenty-Third Publications, 2005 (see Chapter 5).

For Further Reading

Bourg, Florence Caffrey. **Where Two or Three Are Gathered: Christian Families as Domestic Churches**. Notre Dame, IN: University of Notre Dame Press, 2004.

Caldwell, Elizabeth. **Making a Home for Faith: Nurturing the Spiritual Life of Your Children**. Cleveland: United Church Press, 2000.

Garland, Diana. **Family Ministry: A Comprehensive Guide**. Downers Grove, IL: InterVarsity Press, 1999.

— — —. **Sacred Stories of Ordinary Families**. San Francisco: Jossey-Bass, 2003.

Finley, Mitch. **Your Family in Focus**. Notre Dame, IN: Ave Maria Press, 1993.

Finley, Mitch and Kathy Finley. **Building Christian Families**. Allen, TX: Thomas More/Tabor, 1996.

Kehrwald, Leif, editor. **Faith and Families: A Vision and Practice for Parish Ministry**. New London, CT: Twenty-Third Publications, 2006.

Thompson, Margorie. **Family: The Forming Center**. Nashville: Upper Room Books, 1996.

United States Conference of Catholic Bishops. **Follow the Way of Love**. Washington, DC: USCC Publishing, 1994.

Wigger, Bradley. **The Power of God at Home**. San Francisco: Jossey-Bass, 2003.

Appendix 1

The Mission of the Family

EXCERPTS FROM *FOLLOW THE WAY OF LOVE*, 1994
UNITED STATES CONFERENCE OF CATHOLIC BISHOPS

A family is our first community and most basic way in which the Lord gathers us, forms us, and acts in the world. The early Church expressed this truth by calling the Christian family a domestic church or church of the home.

This marvelous teaching was underemphasized for centuries, but reintroduced by the Second Vatican Council. Today we are still uncovering its rich treasure.

The point of the teaching is simple, yet profound. As Christian families, you not only belong to the Church, but your daily life is a true expression of the Church.

Your domestic church is not complete by itself, of course. It should be united with and supported by parishes and other communities within the larger church. Christ has called you and joined you to himself in and through the sacraments. Therefore, you share in one and the same mission that he gives to the whole Church.

You carry out the mission of the church of the home in ordinary ways when:

- You believe in God and that God cares about you.
- You love and never give up believing in the value of another person.
- You foster intimacy, beginning with the physical and spiritual union of the spouses, and extending in appropriate ways to the whole family.
- You evangelize by professing faith in God, acting in accord with Gospel values, and setting an example of Christian living for your children and for others.
- You educate. As the primary teachers of your children, you impart knowledge of the faith and help them to acquire values necessary for Christian living.
- You pray together, thanking God for blessings, reaching for strength, and asking for guidance in crisis and doubt.

- You serve one another, often sacrificing your own wants for the other's good.
- You forgive and seek reconciliation.
- You celebrate life—birthdays and weddings, births and deaths, a first day of school and a graduation, rites of passage into adulthood, new jobs, old friends, family reunions, surprise visits, holy days and holidays. You come together when tragedy strikes and in joyful celebration of the sacraments. As you gather for a meal, you break bread and share stories, becoming more fully the community of love Jesus calls us to be.
- You welcome the stranger, the lonely one, the grieving person into your home. You give drink to the thirsty and food to the hungry. The Gospel assures us that when we do this, they are strangers no more, but Christ.
- You act justly in your community when you treat others with respect, stand against discrimination and racism, and work to overcome hunger, poverty, homelessness, illiteracy.
- You affirm life as a precious gift from God. You oppose whatever destroys life such as abortion, euthanasia, unjust war, capital punishment, neighborhood and domestic violence, poverty and racism.

(United States Conference of Catholic Bishops, *Follow the Way of Love*, p. 8-9)

Chapter Six

Practices of Lifelong Faith Formation

Collaborative and Empowering Leadership for Lifelong Faith Formation

Effective leadership is crucial in facilitating a change of faith formation paradigms. It may well be the most important factor in determining the success or failure of the implementation of lifelong faith formation in a parish community.

Based on our research and experience working with parish teams, we believe that a collaborative and empowering style of leadership is required for lifelong faith formation. This style of leadership needs to be present not just in one person, such as the pastor or director of religious education; it needs to be present in the leadership style of the entire parish staff and ministry teams responsible for fashioning, implementing, and facilitating lifelong faith formation. Since lifelong faith formation is related to every aspect of community life, it requires collaboration among all the various leaders and ministries. Teamwork and collaboration are essential for effective planning and implementation.

How does leadership make a difference in lifelong faith formation? In the Spring of 2005, the Center for Ministry Development conducted a research study, using focus groups and in-depth interviews, of almost 100 parishes in eight dioceses who had been participating in the Generations of Faith project and implementing lifelong faith formation. Analysis of the research identified several important characteristics of the role of leadership in the effective implementation of lifelong faith formation, including the following:

- The participation and investment of the whole parish staff and ministry leaders in lifelong faith formation, not just those involved in faith formation.

- The active support and involvement of the pastor in lifelong faith formation: encouragement, empowering style, long-term commitment, and advocacy.

- The presence of a coordinator who fully understands the vision and can work with others to implement it.

- Effective teams that have a shared vision for implementation and practice teamwork and collaboration.

- A large number of committed volunteer leaders who are engaged in a variety of roles in lifelong faith formation: planning, teaching, organizing, and supporting.

- Volunteer leaders who are empowered and trusted to take responsibility for key aspects of the implementation of lifelong faith formation.

- Concerted efforts to integrate lifelong faith formation with existing parish programs and ministries.

Leadership Teams for Lifelong Faith Formation

Developing and sustaining lifelong faith formation in a parish community involves a variety of leadership teams and collaboration across all the parish's ministries. The research findings point to the necessity of teamwork among the various teams responsible for lifelong faith formation. A team approach is essential because it broadens the base of input into the planning process, and support for the plan and its implementation. The team approach emphasizes collaboration and shared decision-making which builds a strong sense of ownership among team members. This ownership extends the responsibility for faith formation beyond the pastor and director of religious education to all parish leadership, and eventually to the parish community. While the parish's faith formation leaders may take the lead, the involvement of parish staff and ministry leaders is essential. There are four different types of leadership roles involved in lifelong faith formation.

1. The Core Team of parish staff and parish leaders guide the curriculum design process: fashioning a curriculum, implementing a curriculum, and evaluating the curriculum.
2. The Design Team creates the intergenerational learning programs, home activities, and reflection activities for each event.
3. The Implementation Team conducts intergenerational learning programs.
4. Ministry Partners from other parish ministries and programs collaborate with the Core Team on specific projects that involve their particular ministry.

Core Team

The Core Team includes the parish staff, ministry leaders, faith formation leaders, and Catholic school staff. The pastor is an essential member of the Core Team. Their major tasks include:

- promoting and communicating the vision of lifelong faith formation;
- facilitating and sustaining change and innovation in faith formation;
- fashioning the lifelong learning curriculum;
- developing the implementation plan for the lifelong learning curriculum;
- developing leadership for lifelong faith formation by inviting people into leadership, providing training for leaders, and supporting leaders;
- empowering the parish community to recognize its gifts and how to use them in lifelong faith formation;
- coordinating the work of the Design Team and Implementation Team;
- monitoring the progress of the curriculum plan;
- evaluating the implementation of the plan at the end of the year and planning for the next year.

Design Team

The Design Team has the primary responsibility for designing an events-centered learning plan, including an intergenerational program, home faith formation resources, and alignment activities for the whole parish community (embedded, individualized home activities). The Design Team consists of members from the Core Team, especially the parish staff, and other faith formation leaders who are invited to work on the Design Team because of their expertise with particular age groups or particular tasks, such as creating home materials. Their major tasks include:

- designing each intergenerational learning program;
- creating a Home Kit for each event and intergenerational learning program;
- designing reflection activities for the Home Kit;
- selecting and/or designing activities and resources for reaching the whole parish community.

Implementation Team

The Implementation Team has the primary responsibility for conducting intergenerational learning programs. The Implementation Team includes people who will be directly involved in the organization and facilitation of intergenerational learning, and people who will be involved in administrative and support roles. A typical intergenerational learning program will involve a variety of leaders, such as:

- program facilitator or emcee;
- learning group facilitators for age-appropriate learning groups (families with children, adolescents, young adults, adults);
- table group facilitators for age-appropriate learning groups;
- prayer leaders for opening and closing prayer;
- music leader and/or music team for prayer and activities;
- hospitality team;
- set-up and clean-up team;
- food preparation team;
- creative arts people;
- promotion and registration staff.

Ministry Partners

Ministry partners from other parish ministries and programs collaborate with the Core Team, Design Team, and/or Implementation Team on specific projects that involve their particular ministry. For example, the selection of a justice event might involve a number of leaders who are not regularly involved in a leadership role, but are brought into the designing and implementation because of their justice and service expertise.

Ministry partners serve as consultants in design work and resource people for the preparation programs.

Coordinator

When implementing lifelong faith formation, it is essential to have a coordinator(s) who fully understands the vision and can work with others to implement it. In most parishes, one or two people take on the coordination responsibility for lifelong curriculum, facilitating teamwork and managing the process. Without effective teams and teamwork the responsibility for lifelong faith formation can default to one staff member, such as the director of religious education; it is impossible to implement and sustain parish-wide faith formation if it is the responsibility of one person. Appendix 1 provides a list of some of the essential competencies organized by theological knowledge, faith formation knowledge and skills, and leadership skills. While every parish formulates the coordinator's role in response to the needs of the parish community, the suggested competencies can serve as a guide to identifying and/or preparing a coordinator(s) for the work of lifelong faith formation.

Leadership Practices for Lifelong Faith Formation

Collaborative and empowering leadership is part of a paradigm shift in business and organizational life. The findings from parishes implementing lifelong faith formation resonate strongly with the research and writings of management and leadership thinkers. In *The Leadership Challenge*, James Kouzes and Barry Posner identify five practices and ten commitments for leadership drawn from their extensive research with leaders in organizations. They write that leadership is about how leaders mobilize others to want to get extraordinary things done in organizations. "It's about the practices the leaders use to transform values into actions, visions into realities, obstacles into innovations, separateness into solidarity, and risks into rewards" (*The Leadership Challenge*, p. xvii). Their five practices and ten commitments provide specific directions for developing collaborative and empowering leaders in lifelong faith formation.

The following overview introduces the practices and commitments, and provides a tool for leaders to examine their own leadership practices and ways to improve their effectiveness.

Practice 1: Model the Way

Leaders stand for something, believe in something, and care about something. They find their voice by clarifying their personal values, then expressing those values in their own unique and authentic style. Leaders also know that they cannot force their views on others. Instead, they work tirelessly to forge consensus around a set of common principles. Leaders must set the example by aligning their personal actions with shared values. Modeling the way is essentially about earning the right and the respect to lead through direct individual involvement and action. People first follow the person, then the plan.

COMMITMENTS

▶ 1. Find your voice by clarifying your personal values.

▶ 2. Set the example by aligning actions with shared values.

Practice 2. Envision the Future

Leaders envision the future by imaging exciting and ennobling possibilities. They dream of what might be, and they passionately believe they can make a positive difference. They envision the future, creating an ideal and unique image of what the community or organization can become. But the vision of a leader alone is insufficient to mobilize and energize. Leaders must enlist others in exciting possibilities by appealing to shared aspirations. They breathe life into the ideal and unique images of the future and get others to see how their own dreams can be realized by embracing a common vision.

COMMITMENTS

▶ 3. Envision the future by imaging exciting and ennobling possibilities.

▶ 4. Enlist others in a common vision by appealing to shared aspirations.

Practice 3: Challenge the Process

Leaders work for change; to them, the status quo is unacceptable. Leaders search for innovative ways to change, grow, and improve. They seize the initiative to make things happen. And knowing they have no monopoly on good ideas, leaders constantly scan the outside environment for creative ways to do things. Leaders experiment and take risks by constantly generating small wins and by learning from mistakes. And despite persistent opposition and inevitable setbacks, leaders demonstrate the courage to continue the quest. Exemplary leaders know that they have to be willing to make some personal sacrifices in the service of a higher purpose.

COMMITMENTS

▶ 5. Search for innovative ways to change, grow, and improve.

▶ 6. Experiment and take risks by constantly generating small wins and learning from mistakes.

Practice 4: Enable Others to Act

Leaders know they cannot do it alone. It takes partners to get extraordinary things done in an organization. So leaders foster collaboration by promoting cooperative goals and building trust. They develop teams with spirit and cohesion. They promote a sense of reciprocity and a feeling of "we're all in this together." Leaders understand that mutual respect is what sustains extraordinary efforts. Leaders strengthen others by sharing power and providing choice, making each person feel competent and confident. They nurture self-esteem and sustain human dignity.

COMMITMENTS

▶ 7. Foster collaboration by promoting cooperative goals and building trust.

▶ 8. Strengthen others by sharing power and discretion.

Practice 5. Encourage the Heart

Getting extraordinary things done in organizations is hard work. To keep hope and determination alive, leaders need to recognize contributions by showing appreciation for individual excellence. Genuine acts of caring uplift spirits and strengthen courage. On every winning team, the members need to share in the rewards of their efforts, so leaders should celebrate the values and the victories by creating a spirit of community. This means expressing pride in the accomplishments of their team and making everyone feel like everyday heroes.

COMMITMENT

▶ 9. Recognize contributions by showing appreciation for individual excellence.

▶ 10. Celebrate the values and victories by creating a spirit of community.

(This overview of the five practices and ten commitments is summarized from *The Leadership Challenge*, third edition, by James Kouzes and Barry Posner, and *Christian Reflections on the Leadership Challenge*, edited by James Kouzes and Barry Posner.)

Leadership as Stewardship

Collaborative and empowering leadership is rooted in the gospels. Evelyn and James Whitehead propose the gospel image of stewardship as a way to think about Christian leadership.

> In the New Testament and elsewhere, stewardship describes a leadership position reserved for experienced, capable persons. Stewards exercise considerable authority, but not in their own name. Stewardship links power with service (of the community) and authority with dependence (on the Lord). These dynamics describe the exercise of leadership in the contemporary community of faith. (*The Promise of Partnership*, p. 104)

The Whiteheads go on to describe the role of steward in this way:

> Christian leaders are stewards of God's power as it stirs in a community of believers. Leaders are not to do the group's work for it, nor are they single-handedly to supply the group's vision. They do not impart a grace and power that is otherwise lacking here. Their role is to support the group's life in the Spirit. Their task is to foster the network of effective relationships through which members care for one another and pursue shared goals. When they do this, our leaders foster the fruitful flow of God's power among us.
>
> Bringing the group to life and coordinating its power—this is leadership's core. Leadership—or better, leading—goes on in the give-and-take of the whole group. Watching this interplay helps us recognize leadership as a group process more than an individual possession—a process that encompasses all those activities that make a group effective. The formal leader is part of this larger process. Understanding leadership as a group process does not do away with the need for designated leaders. Seeing leadership in this wider view simply clarifies the task of the person in charge. (*The Promise of Partnership*, pp. 104-105)

Flowing from the image of stewardship, the Whiteheads believe that effective leaders act to

1. nurture commitment to a shared vision and common action,
2. enhance the group's power by recognizing their gifts and developing their skills and resources for action, and

3. face the group toward its future by confronting the demands of change and leading transformation.

Leadership as Collaboration

As we have seen, collaboration and teamwork are central to implementing and sustaining lifelong faith formation. Loughlan Sofield and Carroll Juliano describe collaboration as

> the identification, release, and union of all the gifts in ministry for the sake of mission. This definition has three key elements. First, the essence of collaborative ministry is a gift. Second, collaboration is never an end in itself; it is a vehicle for ministry. Third, the goal of collaborative ministry is always the mission of Jesus Christ. (*Collaboration*, p. 17)

Collaboration evolves through a clear, predictable, and developmental process. At level one, *co-existence*, individual leaders or ministry groups within a parish operate separately, independent from one another. Unfortunately this fragmentation is all too common in parish life and can be the result of the old paradigm of faith formation.

At the second level, *communication*, leaders or ministry groups share information with each other, such as programs, activities, and calendars. This initial sharing leads to greater understanding and the recognition of shared purposes and common areas of action. This greater understanding of other ministries is a foundation upon which to build a more collaborative approach, but so far people are only sharing information.

The third level, *cooperation*, is the movement toward interdependence with individuals or groups coordinating schedules and working together on each other's projects. A leader or ministry group gets involved with another ministry or program in the parish community, providing assistance or resources or staff. For example, the youth ministry coordinator recruits young people to serve as leaders in the summer vacation Bible school.

Collaboration is the fourth level, and it presupposes a shared mission among individuals and groups with a desire to work together to achieve a common purpose. There is a spirit of mutuality and partnership, and a valuing of the unique gifts and resources of the partners.

Implementing and sustaining a shared vision of lifelong faith formation requires collaboration among parish leaders and parish ministries toward the common purpose of faith formation for the whole parish community. The development of leadership teams, the practice of effective leadership practices, and the participation of a diversity of leaders and ministries in the processes for fashioning and implementing a life-long curriculum model requires a collaborative approach to ministry. In addition, leaders also need to possess attitudes and skills that nurture collaboration in a parish. Some of the essentials for collaboration include:

- listening and open-mindedness;
- practicing mutual respect, understanding, and trust;
- communicating openly and frequently;
- working together in partnership;
- developing shared responsibility, mutuality, and interdependence;
- developing ownership in both the process and the outcome;
- helping group members see collaboration in their self-interest;
- empowering people to recognize and use their gifts;
- affirming and respecting the gifts of others;
- living servant/stewardship leadership;
- developing skills such as group leadership, conflict resolution, management, confrontation, and discernment of gifts;
- cultivating a collaborative spirituality rooted in the leadership model of Jesus Christ;
- utilizing processes to move a group toward collaboration;
- investing the time and energy in developing a collaborative approach;
- having a skilled facilitator or convener guide the group.

Leadership as Empowering the Gifts of the Community

Churches that are effective in developing leadership—inviting, preparing, and supporting leaders—first embrace an empowering mindset that guides their efforts. These values are rooted in the Christian tradition. In 1 Corinthians 12:4–31, and mirrored in Romans 12 and Ephesians 4, St. Paul offers a vision of Church (body of Christ), of ministry (Spirit-led service to the Church and world), of gifts (given by the Holy Spirit for the building up of the body of Christ), and of mutuality or partnership (complementing gifts, given by the Holy Spirit, for the common good).

These values are echoed in Church teachings:

> The Second Vatican Council has reminded us of the mystery of this power and of the fact that the mission of Christ—Priest, Prophet-Teacher, King—continues in the Church. Everyone, the whole people of God, shares in this threefold mission.

Through the sacraments of baptism, confirmation, and Eucharist, every Christian is called to participate actively and co-responsibly in the Church's mission of salvation in the world. Moreover, in those same sacraments, the Holy Spirit pours out gifts which make it possible for every Christian man and woman to assume different ministries and forms of service that complement one another and are for the good of all.

Everyone has a responsibility to answer the call to mission and to develop the gifts she or he has been given by sharing them in the family, the workplace, the civic community, and the parish or diocese. A parallel responsibility exists within the Church's leadership to acknowledge and foster the ministries, the offices, and the roles of lay faithful that find their foundation in the sacraments of baptism and confirmation, indeed, for a good many of them in the sacrament of matrimony. (*Christifideles Laici* 20, 23)

Inspired by these images from St. Paul and Church teachings, several important values of an empowering mindset emerge.

1. *The Church is the body of Christ; and through our baptism, we are members of the body of Christ.* St. Paul reminds us that each person in the faith community is called to ministry and is blessed with gifts for ministry by the power of the Holy Spirit. In baptism we celebrate the call of each person to ministry within the Church community and the ministry of the church to the world. We believe that each individual brings wonderful gifts to the work of the Church.

Baptism is empowerment. Through baptism, all Christians share in the mission of Christ and the Spirit. The gift of the Spirit at baptism empowers us to fulfill the mission of Jesus Christ. All ministry serves this mission. The baptized serve this mission and share in Christ's priestly, prophetic, and royal office.

The presence of the Spirit of the risen Lord is the source of power in the ministry of the Church. The Church and all its members emerge and draw nourishment from the breaking of the bread, the reality of the resurrection and Pentecost, and the sending forth of the disciples to spread the good news. It is from this perspective that all followers of Jesus share in his ministry.

2. *Individuals and the entire community are blessed with gifts for ministry. Christian ministry is gift-based.* Special charisms of the Holy Spirit, which flow from the sacraments of initiation, equip Christians for their special

tasks within the Church. In the early Church, as needs were recognized in the community, those who were discerned to be appropriately gifted by the Spirit were called forth to serve.

Every aspect of our humanity is intended to serve God's intent for the world. Each person is uniquely gifted for ministry and these gifts consist of more than one's talents. Other aspects of our giftedness include our interests, motivations, values, passions, hopes and dreams, and life journeys. Discernment of gifts must focus on the whole person and the entire context of his or her life: families and friendships, workplaces and schools, neighborhoods and larger communities, and the faith community itself.

3. There is an abundance of gifts for ministry. An abundance mentality means that there is a diversity of gifts already present in the faith community. The Spirit has blessed the community with gifts. There is no shortage of gifts; the primary task of ministry leaders is to facilitate the discovery of these gifts and the utilization of these gifts on behalf of God's kingdom. Some of the gifts will be utilized within parish-based ministries, while others will be exercised in the world.

4. Ministry leaders are called to empower and equip individuals, teams, and, in the end, the entire community to utilize their gifts for the mission of the Church. Ministry leaders are servants to the needs of the community and stewards of the community's resources. They play an essential role in the Church by helping identify the gifts of the community, developing these gifts for ministry, utilizing these gifts on behalf of God's kingdom and the mission of the Church, and supporting the gifts of all Church members. Ministry leaders must be secure enough to equip others for ministry, give them responsibility, and support them as they do their ministry.

What does an empowering mindset mean, in practice, for the development of a leadership strategy for lifelong faith formation? Here are five principles to guide the creation of a leadership strategy.

- Every leadership experience in the Church should encourage a healthy relationship with Jesus Christ. We recognize that leaders have an opportunity to grow in their faith through involvement in ministry. We are concerned about the spiritual growth of leaders and their knowledge and skills for the practice of ministry.
- Leaders are respected as full partners in ministry. We give volunteer leaders responsibility and work with them as team members, sharing the decision-making and work.

- The gifts, abilities, interests, and passions of the leader are honored. We take the time to discern the gifts and talents of leaders and see that the leadership role matches well with their gifts.
- Leaders receive specialized training, resources, and support so that they can adequately perform their ministry, especially when the knowledge or skills involved are new to them. We ensure that volunteer leaders feel capable and confident that they can perform their ministry. We tailor the training and resources to the needs of the leaders and their responsibilities.
- Leaders are appreciated and recognized for the value of their contributions to their ministry and to the Church. We take the time, formally and informally, to express the gratitude of the Church for the work of the volunteer leaders. We create specific strategies, such as dinners, gatherings, rituals, and thank-you notes, to demonstrate appreciation and recognize the contributions of leaders.

A Leadership Strategy

Developing a leadership strategy is one way the parish team practices empowerment. The effective implementation of lifelong faith formation requires a large number of leaders performing a variety of different roles and tasks. Every parish needs to develop a leadership strategy for lifelong faith formation that includes these three major components: 1. inviting people into leadership, 2. preparing and training leaders, and 3. supporting and recognizing leaders. Each of these three components include the following tasks:

1. Inviting people into leadership
   - Identify the leaders you need for lifelong faith formation.
   - Develop job descriptions for each leadership position.
   - Search for persons with leadership potential using parish-wide strategies and personal invitation.
   - Place people in leadership positions.
2. Preparing and training leaders
   - Develop independent learning plans and/or group training for facilitators/teachers for each intergenerational learning program.
   - Conduct a rehearsal meeting for each intergenerational learning program.
   - Evaluate each intergenerational learning program and the performance of the team.

3. Supporting leaders
- Authorize leaders to begin service.
- Provide the information and resources leaders need.
- Gather information and evaluate the work of leaders.
- Express and celebrate the support of the church.

(See Chapter Four in the *Generations of Faith Resource Manual* for the complete process and tools for developing leaders.)

The task of inviting and preparing leaders can be overwhelming, especially in the first years of implementation. It is important to remember that even though lifelong faith formation requires more leaders doing a variety of specific and defined jobs, it also means that the team will be able to involve a greater diversity of the gifts from within the parish community. In the old paradigm, leaders approached the community in search of only teachers or catechists. In the new paradigm, there is a greater diversity of leadership positions so the team will invite people with a variety of gifts: facilitators and teachers, artists and musicians, cooks and hospitality staff, and so on. And no one works alone; everyone is part of a team.

Mentoring new leaders is an important component of a leadership strategy. While the responsibility for the first year of implementing lifelong faith formation rests on current leaders, it is important to begin thinking ahead to the second year, identifying potential leaders who can be mentored into leadership positions. One of the best ways to cultivate new leaders is to partner them with an experienced leader who can gradually develop their knowledge and skills for a leadership position. If every current leader was a mentor to a new leader, there would be a constant source of new leaders for lifelong faith formation.

For example, to develop new facilitators for age-group learning in the monthly intergenerational program, identify people who have great potential but lack knowledge, skills, and/or confidence. Match them with a mentor. Each month they will participate in training, the rehearsal meeting, and the actual intergenerational program. Gradually, over the year, the new leader will take on more and more program responsibility until by the end of the year they are ready to facilitate an age-group learning session. This approach can be applied to all leadership positions. The key is to build the mentoring process into your leadership strategy so that new leaders are always being prepared.

Leadership as Facilitating Change

One of the most difficult realities for parish teams to accept is that a new paradigm for faith formation will take years to become anchored in the life of the parish community.

John Kotter, a Harvard University professor and international consultant on change, says that producing change is about eighty percent leadership—establishing direction, aligning, motivating, and inspiring people—and about twenty percent management—planning, budgeting, organizing, and problem-solving. He has identified eight stages in the change process from his work with organizations of all sizes, both for profit and non-profit.

Kotter says that the first four stages in the transformation process help an organization defrost a hardened status quo. If change were easy, you would not need all the effort. Stages five to seven then introduce many new practices. The last stage grounds the changes in the organizational culture and helps make them stick. Successful change of any magnitude goes through all eight stages, usually in the following sequence. Although one normally operates in multiple phases at once, skipping even a single step and getting too far ahead without a solid base almost always creates problems.

Here are brief descriptions of the eight stages, adapted from John Kotter's book *Leading Change,* that parish leaders and teams can use in conjunction with the processes for fashioning and implementing lifelong faith formation. These steps can serve as guides for planning initiatives to enact change, and for marking progress.

1. Establishing a Sense of Urgency

Establishing a sense of urgency is crucial to gaining needed cooperation. If complacency is high, transformations usually go nowhere because few people are even interested in working toward change. If urgency is low, it's difficult to put together a group with enough power and credibility to guide the effort, to create and communicate a vision for change. Never underestimate the magnitude of the forces that encourage complacency and help maintain the status quo.

STRATEGIES FOR ESTABLISHING A SENSE OF URGENCY

- Examine current realities, that is, the strengths and weaknesses of current approaches to faith formation. What are we doing well? What are the areas we need to improve? Who are we reaching and involving? Who are we not reaching and involving?

- Listen to feedback from parishioners, families, and participants in faith formation programming. What's working for them? What's not? What can be improved?

- Identify recurring problems in faith formation that never seem to get solved. What are the problems that seem to come back each year? What are the problems that no matter how hard we try, we can't seem to solve?

- Identify the major challenges facing the parish and faith formation efforts, both from within and from outside. What are the forces affecting the life of our parish from within the congregation? From the outside community and world? What potential crises do we see looming on the horizon?

- Identify the major opportunities for faith formation that the parish has not acted on yet. What are the positive forces that the parish needs to build on? What are positive trends that could dramatically affect the quality of faith formation?

2. Creating the Guiding Coalition/Team

A strong guiding coalition or team is always needed, one with the right composition, level of trust, and shared objective. Building such a team is an essential part of the early stages of any effort to change. In lifelong faith formation three teams are needed: the core team, design team, and implementation team.

The two key tasks for Stage 2 are

1. to assemble a group with enough power to lead the effort, and

2. to encourage the group to work as a team.

Because leaders are likely to meet resistance from unexpected quarters, building a strong guiding coalition/team is essential. There are three keys to creating such alliances.

- *Engaging the right talent.* The most effective team members usually have strong positional power, broad experience, high credibility, and real leadership skill.

- *Growing the coalition/team strategically.* An effective guiding coalition needs a diversity of views and voices. Once a core group coalesces, the challenge is how to expand the scope and complexity of the coalition. It often means working with people from across the whole parish community.

- *Working as a team, not just a collection of individuals.* Leaders often say they have a team when in fact they have a committee or a small hierarchy. The more you do to support team performance, the healthier the guiding coalition will be and the more able it will be to achieve its goals. Especially during the stress of change, leaders throughout the parish need to draw on reserves of energy, expertise, and, most of all, trust. Real teams are built by doing real work together, sharing a vision, and commitment to a goal.

3. Developing a Vision and Strategy

Vision refers to a picture of the future with some implicit or explicit commentary on why people should strive to create that future. A good vision serves three important purposes. First, by clarifying the general direction for change, it simplifies hundreds of more detailed decisions. Second, it motivates people to take action in the right direction, even if the steps are personally painful or not in people's short-term self-interests. Third, it helps coordinate the actions of different people in a remarkably fast and efficient way. Vision helps align individuals for action.

The two key tasks for Stage 3 are

1. to create a vision to help direct the change effort, and
2. to develop strategies for achieving that vision.

CHARACTERISTICS OF AN EFFECTIVE VISION

- *Imaginable:* conveys a picture of what the future will look like.
- *Desirable:* appeals to the long-term interests of staff, leaders, parishioners, and others who have stake in the parish.
- *Feasible:* comprises realistic, attainable goals.
- *Focused:* is clear enough to provide guidance in decision-making.
- *Flexible:* is general enough to allow individual initiative and alternative responses in light of changing conditions.
- *Communicable:* is easy to communicate; can be successfully explained within five minutes.

4. Communicating the Vision

A great vision can serve a useful purpose even it if is understood by just a few key people. But the real power of a vision is unleashed only when most of the people involved have a common understanding of its goals and direction. That shared sense of desirable future can help motivate and coordinate the kinds of actions that create transformations.

The two key tasks for Stage 4 are

1. to use every vehicle possible to communicate the new vision and strategies, and
2. to teach new behaviors by the example of the guiding coalition.

KEY ELEMENTS IN THE EFFECTIVE COMMUNICATION OF VISION

- *Simplicity:* all jargon must be eliminated.
- *Metaphor, analogy, and example:* a verbal picture is worth a thousand words.
- *Multiple forums:* big meetings and small gatheings, memos and newspapers, formal and informal interaction—all are effective for spreading the word.
- *Repetition:* ideas sink in deeply only after they have been heard many times.
- *Leadership by example:* behavior from important people that is inconsistent with the vision overwhelms other forms of communication.
- *Give-and-take:* two-way communication is always more powerful that one-way communication.

5. Empowering Others to Act on the Vision

Effectively completing Stages 1 through 4 of the transformation process already does a great deal to empower people. But even when urgency is high, a guiding coalition has created an appropriate vision, and the vision has been well communicated, numerous obstacles can still stop leaders from creating needed change. The purpose of Stage 5 is to empower a broad base of people to take action by removing as many barriers to the implementation of the change vision as possible at this point in the process.

The three key tasks for Stage 5 are

1. to get rid of obstacles to change,
2. to change systems or structures that seriously undermine the vision, and
3. to encourage risk taking and non-traditional ideas, activities, and actions.

EMPOWERING PEOPLE TO EFFECT CHANGE

- *Communicate a sensible vision to leaders:* if leaders have a shared sense of purpose, it will be easier to initiate actions to achieve that purpose.

- *Make structures compatible with the vision:* unaligned structures block needed action.
- *Provide the training leaders need:* with the right knowledge, skills, and attitudes, people feel empowered.
- *Align information and personnel systems to the vision:* unaligned systems also block needed action.

6. Planning For and Creating Short-Term Wins

Major change takes time, sometimes lots of time. Zealous believers will often stay the course no matter what happens. Most of the rest expect to see convincing evidence that all the effort is paying off. They want to see clear data indicating that the changes are working and that the change process is not absorbing too many resources in the short-term as to endanger the parish. The three key tasks for Stage 6 are

1. to plan for visible performance improvements,
2. to create those improvements, and
3. to recognize leaders involved in the improvements.

A good short-term win has at least these three characteristics:

1. It's visible; large numbers of people can see for themselves whether the result is real or just hype;
2. It's unambiguous; there can be little argument over the call;
3. It's clearly related to the change effort.

THE ROLE OF SHORT-TERM WINS

- *Provide evidence that sacrifices are worth it:* wins greatly help justify the short-term costs involved.
- *Reward change agents with a pat on the back:* after a lot of hard work, positive feedback builds morale and motivation.
- *Help fine-tune vision and strategies:* short-term wins give the guiding coalition concrete data on the viability of their ideas.
- *Undermine cynics and self-serving resisters:* clear improvements in performance make it difficult for people to block needed change.
- *Keep key leaders and councils on board:* provides those in leadership positions in the organization with evidence that the transformation is on track.
- *Build momentum:* turns neutrals into supporters, reluctant supporters into active helpers.

7. Consolidating Improvements and Producing More Change

When a project is completed or an initial goal met, it is tempting to congratulate all involved and proclaim the advent of a new era. While it is important to celebrate results along the way, kidding yourself or others about the difficulty and duration of organizational transformation can be catastrophic. People look forward to the completion of any task. The problem is, the results of a change are not directly proportional to the effort invested. That is, one-third of the way into a process of change, the leadership team is unlikely to see one-third of the possible results. They may only see ten percent of the possible results. If the team settles for too little too soon, they will probably lose it all. Celebrating incremental improvements is a great way to mark progress and sustain commitment—but don't forget how much work is still to come. There is one cardinal rule: whenever you let up before the job is done, critical momentum can be lost and regression may follow.

The three major tasks of Stage 7 are

1. to use increased credibility to change systems, structures, and policies that do not fit the vision,
2. to develop leaders who can implement the vision, and
3. to reinvigorate the process with new projects and themes.

What Stage 7 Looks Like in a Successful, Major Change Effort

- *More change, not less:* the guiding coalition uses the credibility afforded by short-term wins to tackle additional and bigger projects.
- *More help:* additional people are recruited and developed to help implement the changes.
- *Leadership from senior management (parish staff/core team):* leaders focus on maintaining the clarity of a shared purpose for the overall effort, and keeping urgency levels up.
- *Project management and leadership from other leaders and teams (implementation teams and ministry partners):* those involved in development and implementation of change (programs) provide leadership for specific projects and manage those projects.

8. Anchoring (Institutionalizing) New Approaches in the Culture

Culture refers to norms of behavior and shared values among a group of people. Norms of behavior are common or pervasive ways of acting that are found in a group. They persist because group members tend to behave in ways that teach these practices to new members, rewarding those who fit it and sanctioning those who do not. Values that are shared by most of the people in a group tend to shape group behavior, which often persists over time, even when group membership changes.

Culture is not something that can be easily manipulated. Attempts to grab it and twist it into a new shape never work because you cannot grab it. A culture changes only after you have successfully altered people's actions, after new patterns of behavior produce some group benefit for a period of time, and after people see the connection between the new actions and an improvement in performance. Thus most cultural change happens in Stage 8, not Stage 1.

The two major tasks of Stage 8 are

1. to articulate the connections between the new behaviors and organizational success, and

2. to develop the means to ensure leadership development and succession.

ANCHORING CHANGE IN A CULTURE

- *Comes last, not first:* most alterations in norms and shared values come at the end of the transformation process.

- *Depends on results:* new approaches usually sink into a culture only after it's very clear that they work and are superior to old methods.

- *Requires a lot of talk:* without verbal instruction and support, people are often reluctant to admit the validity of new practices.

- *May involve turnover:* sometimes the only way to change a culture is to change key people.

- *Makes decisions on leadership development and succession crucial:* if the development of new staff and new leaders are not changed to be compatible with the new practices, the old culture will reassert itself.

Over time the changes will become anchored in the life of the parish community, and people will say: "We've always done faith formation this way." But change takes time! Here are several indicators that the lifelong faith formation paradigm is becoming anchored in your parish community:

- There is lots of "buzz" among participants, who are now bringing new individuals and families to the intergenerational learning program. People who were once marginal to faith formation and parish life are now getting involved.

- The curriculum plan moves into its third or fourth year and is now fully implemented.

- New learning models (intergenerational learning, alignment of learning across the whole parish) gain wider acceptance and participation.

- There is a wider use of home activities, as evidenced through stories and evaluation.

- The job descriptions of parish staff and key leaders are modified to embrace the work change required by lifelong faith formation.

- Parish catechetical policies and handbooks are revised to incorporate the lifelong faith formation vision and practices.

- The orientation program for new staff members includes an orientation about lifelong faith formation.

Leadership as Nurturing Adoption of the Innovation

When making an innovation—and lifelong faith formation is an innovation—everyone seems to ask, "But really, how long will it take for people to get on board?" The hard reality is that the adoption of lifelong faith formation by the parish community takes time, and nobody knows how long it will take. It is important to realize that the parish community is making an innovation. It is changing paradigms and embracing lifelong faith formation. This introduces four innovative practices to the parish community: an events-centered, lifelong curriculum for all generations, intergenerational learning, household faith formation, and, for some, renewed participation in parish life.

Yet, there are patterns in the adoption of an innovation that parish leaders can use to facilitate the adoption process. Everett Rogers (*The Diffusion of Innovations*) has studied the process of adoption for products and ideas in a diversity of populations. Certain patterns have emerged.

First, Rogers found that perceptions concerning an innovation are crucial to the diffusion process. Five characteristics influence the adoption or rejection of an innovation.

1. *Relative advantage,* the degree to which the innovation is perceived as being better than the idea it supercedes. (How do the benefits of the innovation outweigh the current approach and its problems?)

2. *Compatibility,* or the perception that the innovation is consistent with existing values, past experiences, and the needs of potential adopters; being able to connect it to a previous tradition or way of doing things is important and provides an anchor to people's

meanings. (How does the innovation connect to the parish mission and values?)

3. *Complexity,* or the degree to which the innovation is perceived as difficult to understand and use. (How is the innovation simpler to understand and use—more user-friendly?)

4. *Trialability,* or the degree to which the innovation may be experimented with on a limited basis; think of the trial as a way to gradually internalize the innovation. (How do we provide people with the opportunity to experience it first before they make a commitment?)

5. *Observability,* which is the degree to which the results of an innovation are visible to others. (How do we make sure that we don't just talk about the innovation, but actually implement it so that people can see it and experience it?)

Second, Rogers says that it takes time for an innovation to reach critical mass, the point at which enough individuals have adopted it so that its further rate of adoption is self-sustaining. Reaching critical mass will usually take longer than most parishes are willing to commit to, and resistance may be strongest right before critical mass is achieved. To be diffused, innovation takes time and resources; it demands commitment from parish leadership to stay the course. The wise investment of resources requires an emphasis on the *journey* to achieve critical mass.

Third, Rogers found that people differ markedly in their readiness to try new ideas, concepts, and programs. People can be classified into adopter categories (see below). The adoption process is represented as a normal distribution when plotted over time. After a slow start, an increasing number of people adopt the innovation, the number reaches a peak, and then it diminishes as fewer nonadopters remain. Innovators are defined as the first 2.5% of the people to adopt a new idea; the early adopters are the next 13.5% who adopt the new idea; early majority constitute 34% of the total population. Eventually the late majority (34%) adopt the innovation. The laggards represent 16%, and may or may not adopt the innovation.

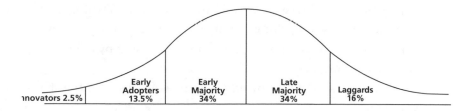

Rogers sees the five groups as differing in their value orientation. Innovators are venturesome; they are willing to try new ideas at some risk. Early adopters are guided by respect; they are opinion leaders in their community and adopt new ideas early but carefully. The early majority are deliberate; they adopt new ideas before the average person, although they rarely are leaders. The late majority are skeptical; they adopt an innovation only after a majority of people have tried it. Finally, laggards are tradition bound; they are suspicious of changes, mix with other tradition-bound people, and adopt the innovation only when it takes on a measure of tradition itself.

It is very important that leaders target each group with the invitation and message that will work for them. It is also important to note that adoption (and therefore change) moves from left to right: from innovators to early adopters to the majority. One group "evangelizes" the next group.

We can see this process at work with consumer goods. Think of the process of adoption as applied to the acceptance and purchase of DVD players. In the beginning, adoption is slow with only the innovators, such as movie lovers and those with home entertainment systems, purchasing high-priced DVD players. Slowly more and more people are exposed to DVD players, more movies are produced in DVD format, sales increase, prices drop, and the innovation grows. It took almost a decade, but today, the DVD is not only the preferred format for movies, it is the *only* format, and DVD players are everywhere. Now that's adoption!

As more and more members of the parish community adopt the innovation (participate in intergenerational learning and Church life, engage in household faith sharing), the innovation becomes anchored in the parish community and spreads more widely. Adoption moves deliberately through these audiences over time. It will take time for the new paradigm to gain acceptance, but it is happening in parish communities all across the country. Adoption and change take time!

Conclusion

In contemporary leadership thinking, collaborative and empowering leadership is the norm. What have we learned about leadership?

1. Leaders have a compelling vision of the future that they believe in.
2. Leaders forge a consensus around a shared vision by appealing to shared aspirations.
3. Leaders model the way by aligning their actions with the shared vision.

4. Leaders align structure, systems, and operational processes to achieve the vision and plan.

5. Leaders innovate and take risks, seizing the initiative to act

6. Leaders enable others to act by empowering people to recognize and use their gifts, and by providing the training and resources leaders need to succeed.

7. Leaders foster collaboration by promoting cooperative goals, building trust, and sharing power.

8. Leaders encourage the heart by recognizing contributions of team members and celebrating the values and victories of the team.

9. Leaders are stewards, linking their power with service and their authority with dependence on the Lord.

10. Leaders bring the group to life and coordinate its power, recognizing that leadership is a group process.

11. Leaders demonstrate collaboration by practicing mutual respect, understanding, and trust, and communicating openly and frequently.

12. Leaders develop the skills for collaboration and teamwork: group leadership, conflict resolution, management, confrontation, and discernment of gifts.

13. Leaders facilitate the change process and nurture innovation through predictable steps over time.

Most importantly, leaders and teams put their trust in Jesus Christ and seek to make him their model and guide for leadership.

Works Cited

Pope John Paul II. **Christifideles Laici**. Washington, DC: USCCB Publishing, 1988.

Kotter, John. **Leading Change**. Cambridge, MA: Harvard Business School Press, 1996.

Kouzes, James and Barry Posner. **The Leadership Challenge**, third edition. San Francisco: Jossey-Bass, 2002.

Kouzes, James and Barry Posner, editors. **Christian Reflections on the Leadership Challenge**. San Francisco: Jossey-Bass, 2004.

Rogers, Everett. **The Diffusion of Innovations** (fifth edition). New York: The Free Press, 2003.

Sofield, Loughlan and Carroll Juliano. **Collaboration: Uniting Our Gifts in Ministry**. Notre Dame, IN: Ave Maria Press, 2000.

Whitehead, James and Evelyn Eaton Whitehead. **The Promise of Partnership**. San Francisco: Harper and Row, 1991.

For Further Reading

Hiesberger, Jean Marie. **Fostering Leadership Skills in Ministry**. Liguori, MO: Liguor Publications, 2003.

Kotter, John. **Leading Change**. Cambridge, MA: Harvard Business School Press, 1996.

Kotter, John and Dan S. Cohen. **The Heart of Change: Real-Life Stories of How People Change Their Organizations**. Cambridge, MA: Harvard Business School Press, 2002.

Kouzes, James and Barry Posner. **The Leadership Challenge** (third edition). San Francisco: Jossey-Bass, 2002.

Kouzes, James and Barry Posner, editors. **Christian Reflections on the Leadership Challenge**. San Francisco: Jossey-Bass, 2004.

Sofield, Loughlan and Carroll Juliano. **Collaboration: Uniting Our Gifts in Ministry**. Notre Dame, IN: Ave Maria Press, 2000.

Whitehead, James and Evelyn Eaton Whitehead. **The Promise of Partnership**. San Francisco: Harper and Row, 1991.

Appendix 1

A Guide to the Role of a Lifelong Faith Formation Coordinator

In most parishes one or two people take on the coordination responsibility for the lifelong learning curriculum. While every parish formulates the coordinator's role in response to the needs of the parish community, here are some of the essential competencies organized by theological knowledge, faith formation knowledge and skills, and leadership skills. This can serve as guide to identifying and/or preparing a coordinator(s) for the work of lifelong faith formation.

Theological Knowledge
- An understanding of the theology, symbols, history, and tradition of the Church year.
- An understanding of the theology, symbols, rituals, and history of the sacraments.
- An understanding of the biblical and theological foundations of Catholic social teaching and of the principles of Catholic social teaching.
- Familiarity with the key teachings of the *Catechism of the Catholic Church* on creed, sacraments, morality, justice, prayer, and spirituality.
- An understanding the scriptural-theological content of the events and learning programs in the parish's curriculum plan: Church year feasts or seasons, sacraments, justice and service projects, prayer practices, and spiritual traditions.

Faith Formation Knowledge and Skills
- Familiarity with the vision and practice of lifelong faith formation and its grounding in the *General Directory for Catechesis*.
- Ability to design and facilitate intergenerational learning.
- Ability to work with families and a variety of age groups from childhood through older adulthood.

- Ability to use a variety of resources in faith formation, such as print, media, and Internet resources.
- Ability to design an events-centered learning plan: intergenerational learning programs, home materials, and reflection activities.
- Familiarity with learning styles, multiple intelligences, and experiential learning, as well as their application to events-centered learning.
- Comfort in using the Internet as a resource for faith formation and leadership training.

Leadership Skills

- An ability to convene a leadership group, representing a variety of ministries, to fashion and sustain a lifelong, events-centered curriculum plan.
- An ability to facilitate the work of a team in developing an events-centered learning plan: design of preparation programs for all ages and generations, home materials, and reflection activities.
- An ability to work collaboratively in the implementation of a curriculum plan and intergenerational learning program.
- An ability to develop a leadership system for identifying, training, and supporting faith formation leaders.
- An ability to provide training for leaders.

Becoming a Church of Lifelong Learners

We are at the beginning of a major transformation in faith formation in the Catholic Church. Parishes large and small, urban and suburban, big city and small town, multi-ethnic and multi-lingual are embracing and implementing events-centered, lifelong intergenerational faith formation.[1] Our understanding of the theory and practice of lifelong faith formation continues to develop as more and more parishes make the paradigm shift. Positive signs of the growth of a new paradigm are seen in the growing number of articles and books, intergenerational program resources and materials written for the home.[2] One only needs to look back to the mid-1990s to realize how much progress has been made. Still, we are at the early stages of the paradigm shift to lifelong faith formation.

This book is an attempt to articulate the vision and practices for lifelong faith formation as it is developing out of the thinking of religious educators: the paradigm pioneers, the catechetical vision of the Catholic Church in the *General Directory for Catechesis* and the *National Directory for Catechesis,* and the experiences of parishes implementing lifelong faith formation. As we have seen, the emerging vision that is guiding the transformation of parish formation has the following characteristics:

- nurturing the Catholic identity of all parishioners for a lifetime;
- utilizing the whole life of the Church as its faith formation curriculum, that is, Church year feasts and seasons, sacraments, liturgy, justice and service, prayer and spirituality, community life;
- re-engaging all generations in participating in Catholic community life, especially Sunday Mass;

- involving all of the generations in learning together through intergenerational learning;

- equipping and supporting families, and especially parents, in creating a pattern of family faith sharing and a Catholic way of life;

- addressing the hungers of the post-Vatican II Catholics for experience, participation, interaction, connection, community, spirituality, meaning, and practices for living;

- transforming the parish community into a community of lifelong learners, engaging everyone as both teacher and learner.

A new vision requires a new set of practices to bring the vision to life. We have proposed four practices to give shape and form to the vision. These practices are designed so parishes can apply the vision to the unique culture and character of their parish community. All four practices are essential to the effective implementation of lifelong faith formation.

- Practice 1. Events-centered curriculum for the whole parish community.

- Practice 2. Events-centered intergenerational learning.

- Practice 3. Household faith formation.

- Practice 4. Collaborative and empowering leadership.

What Are We Learning?

Even though we are at the early stages of the paradigm shift, we can observe trends in the experience of parishes that are implementing lifelong faith formation through the Generations of Faith project. From our experience working with parishes and from their own stories we can identify several ways lifelong faith formation is having an impact on the parish community.

- Parishes are having success in engaging all ages in faith formation, especially parents and adults of all ages. They now have a lifelong curriculum that provides foundational catechesis for everyone.

- Parishes are discovering that a events-centered, lifelong curriculum is a systematic and thorough presentation of the foundations of the Catholic faith. Many parishes have shifted their catechetical model entirely to the events-centered curriculum, introducing monthly intergenerational learning programs for the whole parish community and eliminating weekly age-group classes.

- Parishioners of all ages are developing a deeper understanding of the foundational themes of the Catholic faith—Church year, liturgy, sacraments, creed, morality, prayer, justice—and at the same time, learning how to live their faith in the parish, at home, and in the world.

- Parishes are seeing a direct connection between preparing people for a Church event and their participation in the event. This approach is beginning to re-engage people of all ages in parish life.
- Parishes are having success with the intergenerational learning model, gathering parishioners of all generations to learn together. Many parishes are overwhelmed by the high level of participation and the positive response from parishioners of all ages, especially middle-aged adults without children and older adults.
- Parishioners are beginning to build relationships with people across all ages, and this is benefiting the entire parish community.
- Parents are participating in faith formation with their children, often for the first time, and they are finding a benefit in learning together as a family. Families are beginning to incorporate faith sharing activities at home.
- Parishioners of all ages are finding ways to use the activities in the Home Kit as part of their daily life.
- Parish teams across ministries are working together to design and conduct intergenerational faith formation sessions. Lifelong faith formation is bringing parish leaders together in a common effort to implement lifelong faith formation.

Many of our observations of these trends in parish communities have been confirmed by a research study in the Spring of 2005 with almost 100 parishes, in eight dioceses, who have been participating in the Generations of Faith Project. Each parish in the study is presenting events-centered intergenerational learning programs on a monthly or seasonal basis.

Using focus groups and in-depth interviews, the following findings emerged to describe the experience and learning of a diversity of parishes practicing lifelong faith formation. They are organized into three groups: factors that influenced a parish's readiness for lifelong faith formation, factors that concerned leadership for lifelong faith formation, and factors that made for effective intergenerational learning.[3]

Readiness Findings

1. Parish leaders hoped that lifelong faith formation would provide a way for families to learn and share faith together both at the parish and at home.

2. Parish leaders hoped that lifelong faith formation would increase participation in the events and ministries of the parish.

3. Parishes realized that the classroom model of faith formation did not work well in their parishes.

4. Parishes identified a number of factors already present in parishes that contributed to their readiness to move toward lifelong faith formation: experience with family programming; an empowering mindset on the part of leaders; good liturgy; hunger for learning; the confidence of the parish community in the parish leader; and a willingness on the part of parish leadership to try new things.

Leadership Findings

1. Successful implementation of lifelong faith formation depends on the paticipation and investment of the whole parish staff and ministry leaders in lifelong faith formation, not just those involved in faith formation.

2. The active support and involvement of the pastor, as evidenced by encouragement, an empowering style, long-term commitment, and advocacy, is important for the effective implementation of lifelong faith formation.

3. It is essential to have a coordinator who fully understands the vision and can work with others to implement it.

4. Successful implementation of lifelong faith formation involves concerted efforts to integrate lifelong faith formation with all existing parish programs and ministries.

5. Effective teams have a shared vision for implementation, and practice teamwork and collaboration.

6. Lifelong faith formation requires a large number of committed volunteer leaders, and parishes are discovering talented and resourceful people in their community.

7. A large number of committed volunteer leaders are engaged in a variety of roles in lifelong faith formation: planning, teaching, organizing, and supporting.

8. Volunteer leaders are empowered and trusted to take responsibility for key aspects of the implementation of lifelong faith formation.

9. Through their participation as leaders in lifelong faith formation, leaders feel closer to God, and grow in their knowledge of the Catholic faith and their confidence in sharing it with others.

Intergenerational Learning Findings

1. There is involvement of all ages and generations—parents, children, teens, young adults, adults, older adults, and whole families—in faith formation through intergenerational learning. It is still a challenge to involve certain groups in the parish, such as Catholic school families, young adults, and single adults.

2. Intergenerational relationships are created as people of all ages learn from each other and grow in faith together.

3. Intergenerational learning strengthens the parish community through relationship-building and participation in parish life. People take time to talk and share with each other.

4. Participation in intergenerational learning leads to greater involvement in parish life, including the liturgical and sacramental life of the parish, justice and service projects, and parish ministries.

5. Intergenerational learning addresses a hunger adults have to learn more about their faith and fill in the gaps in their formation. More adults are participating in faith formation.

6. Families enjoy opportunities to pray, learn, and be together. Families are growing in the ways in which they share faith.

7. Intergenerational learning creates an environment in which participants feel safe to learn, ask questions, and grow in faith.

8. Participants are engaged in a variety of learning activities that are experiential, multi-sensory, and interactive. Faith sharing and personal experience are an important element of learning.

9. Adequate parish meeting space plays a key role in conducting successful intergenerational learning programs.

10. Intergenerational learning is exciting: the enthusiasm, joy, and energy are attractive and contagious.

Hope for the Future

We live in times that present urgent challenges for developing a Catholic way of life and sharing our Catholic faith with the next generation. Yet we do not come empty-handed to these challenges. We are building a new paradigm from the wisdom learned over the past forty years from the pioneers of faith formation in the Catholic Church. Even though we are taking the first steps on the journey toward a new paradigm and there is still much more to learn, we can see hopeful, positive signs from parish leaders and parishioners on the impact of lifelong faith formation in their parish community. These parishes are pioneering a new future for Catholic faith formation.

As we close, our attention focuses on the next generations of Catholics—our children, grandchildren, and great-grandchildren. How can we create faith formation that engages them, develops their Catholic identity, and empowers them to live the Catholic way of life? Our answer to this question will be our legacy to them. In *The Church in the Modern World* (*Gaudium et Spes*) the Council Fathers remind us "the future of humanity lies in the hands of those who are strong enough to provide coming generations with reasons for living and hoping" (32). Through the grace of God, may we meet this challenge.

End Notes

1. For more information about lifelong faith formation and stories about parishes implementing lifelong faith formation go to www.generationsoffaith.org.

2. Since 2000 there has been a dramatic increase in writing about catechesis for the whole parish and resources for intergenerational learning and household faith formation. See for example:

> Anslinger, Leisa. *Here Comes Everybody: Whole Community Catechesis in the Parish*. New London, CT: Twenty-Third Publications, 2004.
>
> Huebsch, Bill. *Whole Community Catechesis in Plain English*. New London, CT: Twenty-Third Publications, 2002.
>
> Huebsch, Bill. *The Handbook for Success in Whole Community Catechesis*. New London, CT: Twenty-Third Publications, 2004.
>
> Martineau, Mariette. *People of Faith Organizer's Manual*. Orlando, FL: Harcourt Religion, 2005.
>
> Roberto, John. *Generations of Faith Resource Manual*. New London, CT: Twenty-Third Publications, 2005.

The *People of Faith* series from Harcourt Religion (www.harcourtreligion.com) provides intergenerational programs and magazines for the home. The first six titles in the series include:

> *Acting for Justice* (2005)
>
> *Following Jesus* (2005)
>
> *Professing Our Faith* (2006)
>
> *Celebrating Sacraments* (2006)
>
> *Responding in Prayer* (2006)
>
> *Living the Moral Life* (2007)

3. You can obtain a copy of the Generations of Faith research study by going to www.generationsoffaith.org, and downloading or printing a PDF copy of the report.

Contents for the CD-ROM

1. Article Reprints

Chapter Two traces the development of the lifelong, Church-centered paradigm of faith formation through the work of C. Ellis Nelson, John Westerhoff, Berard Marthaler, Maria Harris, Charles Foster, and Catherine Dooley. To gain a deeper understanding of their thinking, the following essays from their books and journal articles are presented on the CD-ROM. Each of these essays provides a glimpse of the contribution that each religious educator has made to the development of a new paradigm for faith formation. To read more about these religious educators consult the bibliography at the end of the Chapter Two.

Also included are essays by Ann Marie Mongoven on the development of the catechetical vision of the Catholic Church through its major documents since Vatican II, by Robert Duggan on the implications of the *General Directory for Catechesis* for faith formation, by Bill Huebsch on whole community catechesis, and by Joseph White on intergenerational religious education.

Dooley, Catherine. "Renewing the Parish." **Living Light,** Volume 40, Number 1 (Fall 2003).

— — —. "Liturgical Catechesis for Confirmation." **Traditions and Transitions**. Edited by Eleanor Bernstein, CSJ and Martin Connell. Chicago: LTP, 1998. (pp. 253-265)

— — —. "Mystagogy: A Model for Sacramental Catechesis." **The Candles Are Still Burning**. Edited by Mary Grey, Andree Heaton, and Danny Sullivan. Collegeville, MN: Liturgical Press, 1995. (Chapter 6, pp. 58-69)

Duggan, Robert. "The New Constellation of Catechesis." **Living Light**, Volume 37, Number 4 (Summer 2001).

Foster, Charles. "Congregational Events." **Embracing Diversity**. Washington, DC: Alban Institute, 1997. (Chapter 5)

— — —. "Events that Form and Transform." **Educating Congregations**. Nashville: Abingdon, 1994. (Chapter 2)

— — —. "The Faith Community as a Guiding Image for Christian Education." **Contemporary Approaches to Christian Education**. Edited by Jack L. Seymour and Donald E. Miller. Nashville: Abingdon Press, 1982.

Huebsch, Bill. "Principles of Whole Community Catechesis." (Unpublished)

Harris, Maria. "Church: A People with an Educational Vocation." **Fashion Me a People: Curriculum in the Church.** Louisville, KY: Westminister/John Knox Press, 1989. (Chapter 2)

Marthaler, Berard. "Socialization as Model for Catechetics." **Foundations of Religious Education**. Edited by Padraic O'Hare. New York: Paulist Press, 1978. (pp. 64-92)

Mongoven, Anne Marie. "The Story of Affirmation: 1971-1997 Church Documents on Catechesis." **The Prophetic Spirit of Catechesis**. New York: Paulist Press, 2000. (pp. 64-86)

Nelson, C. Ellis. "Socialization Revisited." **Union Seminary Quarterly Review,** Volume 47, Numbers 3-4 (1993).

Westerhoff, John. "In Search of Community." **Will Our Children Have Faith?** (Revised Edition) New York: Morehouse Publishing, 2000. (Chapter 3)

Westerhoff, John and Gwen Kennedy Neville. "Protestants and Roman Catholics Together," and "What is Religious Socialization." **Generation to Generation**. Philadelphia: United Church Press, 1974. (Chapter 1 and Chapter 2)

White, Robert. "IGRE is...(an Exposition of Terms)." **Intergenerational Religious Education**. Birmingham, AL: Religious Education Press, 1988.

2. PowerPoint Presentations

The CD-ROM also includes six PowerPoint presentations with the key concepts and examples from each chapter.

Presentation 1 (Chapter 1) - Reading the Signs of the Times

Presentation 2 (Chapter 2) - A Vision of Lifelong Faith Formation

Presentation 3 (Chapter 3) - Events-Centered Systematic Curriculum

Presentation 4 (Chapter 4) - Intergenerational Learning

Presentation 5 (Chapter 5) - Family and Household Faith Formation

Presentation 6 (Chapter 6) - Collaborative and Empowering Leadership